Right
From
Wrong

Right From Wrong

My Story of Guilt and Redemption

Jacob Dunne

Harper
North

HarperNorth
Windmill Green
Mount Street
Manchester M2 3NX

A division of
HarperCollins*Publishers*
1 London Bridge Street
London SE1 9GF

www.harpercollins.co.uk

HarperCollins*Publishers*
Macken House, 39/40 Mayor Street Upper,
Dublin 1, D01 C9W8

First published by HarperNorth in 2022
This edition published by HarperNorth in 2023

1 3 5 7 9 10 8 6 4 2

A catalogue record for this book
is available from the British Library

PB ISBN: 978-0-00-847214-6

Printed and bound in Great Britain by
CPI Group (UK) Ltd, Croydon

For James

And for Jess, Xander and Tiggy

Contents

Prologue

I want you to be in no doubt that the Meadows Estate, where I grew up and still lived until last year, is the permanent backdrop and the lens through which I have viewed the majority of my life up to and including now. The context for every grubby insight into the intricacies of low-level drug dealing, every skewed nuance of Nottingham gang culture and for every self-pitying recollection of what it's like to suddenly find yourself in prison at the age of 19.

On some level, I hate the place. Part of me wants to forget the house on the corner of Bathley Street where I spent my childhood. I used to find little baggies of drugs on the pavement outside it as I walked to the bus stop to go to primary school. At the time I had no idea what they were. A few years later I'd be dealing them by the ounce for money to buy clothes and booze.

Then there was the road to the side of our house where some nutjob set fire to a car during my ninth birthday party. The parents of my friends from a different (better) part of town looked on in a mixture of disbelief and horror when they came to pick up their kids. I can hardly blame them. The nine-year-old me was becoming accustomed to crime, and particularly the sound of early morning police raids on the street. Ten years later it would be my mum's house being raided and I would be to blame.

Given everything I've been through, the desire to leave The Meadows and forget about it has never really disappeared, and now I've had a glimpse of what else there is. Recently, I've been thinking of moving away – escaping to a Victorian semi in another part of the city, with high ceilings and grand fireplaces. Or perhaps even further. Not everyone gets that chance.

But there's another side of me that I just can't deny. It's the part that acknowledges my heritage – the environment that formed me, for better or worse. In some way I appreciate the desolate grey concrete, the underpasses that smell of piss, the lines of alcoholics outside the pub, and the corner at the end of our road where, even today as I take my kids for a walk, you'll see teenage lads circling on pushbikes dealing drugs. And I have a lot of respect for the people who live in this place. There are plenty of people in more pain and stress than they can manage.

I like to think of them as broken souls, pulling each other further and further down into the abyss, not because they want to be there, but because they just don't know how to do anything else. Every other week I read about an assault, a stabbing or even a murder in The Meadows.

When I learn more about these stories, most of them are familiar. I've heard them before – from cellmates or friends who were in gangs – or I have witnessed the same thing myself. There is no excuse for violence, drugs and murder. People who commit such acts should expect to face the judicial system, just like I did.

But that doesn't make them inhuman. The other day a drug dealer, noticing my son approaching on his bike, bent down to his level with a beaming grin on his face, not to offer him drugs, but to tell him how well he was doing learning to ride it. I couldn't help smiling as we walked away. Even in the hearts of drug dealers, you will find a code of human decency if you look hard enough.

Obviously, I completely relate to all of this. I I know full well how a few bad choices can lead to tragic circumstances. It is sad how attractive and appealing criminality can be when you have no direction and no hope – only a festering disdain for a system that offered people like me nothing other than what they were born into: a substandard existence in an English housing estate whose inhabitants did nothing but perpetuate this fatalistic view of the world.

What about today?

Well, I'm worlds apart from the person I'm describing here, but that has taken this entire book to try and put into words. I had even less direction and hope after I was released from prison than before I went in. The Nottingham riots raged at the time, as if to mirror my own self-destruction. Post-prison me was such a shell of a young man, with raging resentment, newly learned insights into how to commit crime, and the more immediate problem of having nowhere to live. I could have easily headed back to my old haunts and rekindled toxic friendships.

But I didn't.

Instead I started to trust.

I trusted in the idea that by getting the education I'd squandered, it would serve me well. I completely bought into the idea that Restorative Justice (RJ) – a process of rehabilitation and reconciliation – could not only offer great comfort to my victim's family, but also help me repair myself. I trusted that by being responsible and doing the best, one day I could create the kind of nurturing family environment that I lacked. I've never stopped trusting, and as much as I remind myself in low moments along the way that I still rely on the kindness of others, I feel that I've got something to offer the world. I hope this book can help me say it.

Chapter One

The Meadows

I hadn't thought about much of my childhood until recently. In truth I struggle to remember as much as I would like to. Part of the reason that I chose to write a book now is to try and remember more of these happy times – and to honour the rare precious memories that I am scared of forgetting for good.

The sad reality is that the story I tell publicly is predominantly focused on the tragic things I have experienced in my life and the one awful act I committed that ended someone else's.

I now feel like one of the elders in my family. Over the last few years, my mum, her twin sister and Nan have all passed away. I have been so busy trying to right wrongs of the world that I have hardly had a moment to honour these women who raised me. Each of them was important in their own way. All of them loved me dearly and showed it.

When considering my mum's upbringing, I don't think I have ever appreciated what life must have been like for her being adopted. Her adopted father Deryck died of cancer when my

1

mum was in her late teens so she only had her 'mum' and two 'sisters' left in what was already a very small family.

Because of that, my Aunty Paula spent a lot of time with us while we were growing up. She had two children of her own who are of a similar age to me and the upshot of that was that my cousins were and are more like my siblings really – sharing many of our celebrations: caterpillar cakes, water-bomb fights, punctured bike tyres and train journeys to good old Skegness. In those days summer breaks seemed to last a lifetime and the simplest of games could keep us all amused for hours. Without wishing to sound too old and wistful, that was the best time.

I also have an Aunty Julie – we saw a bit less of her because she was the bright one who had gone to university and married a solicitor, my Uncle John. They lived in West Bridgford, the posh suburb on the other side of Trent Bridge.

I lived for almost all my life in our three-bedroomed house in Nottingham's Meadows estate on a corner plot with an unusually large garden, but I was actually born near Liverpool, on the Wirral.

At the time, my dad was working as a painter and decorator and my mum was a lifeguard at a local leisure centre. It was there that they met, with my mum eventually moving in almost without discussion – dad says he arrived home from work one day to see my mum pottering around with dinner on the go. A year or so later I was born. They soon moved from the North West, away from my dad's family, and settled in Nottingham.

Given how young I was, I have no recollection of the place where I was born. Many years later – I was probably 12 at the time – my mum, my brother Sam, my two cousins and I went there on a day-trip pilgrimage.

We looked at the house on the Wirral, walked along the street, and then I just remember standing around on the flood defences, moaning like any good teenager might about how cold it was, while the younger kids ran around and played on the sand below.

We dashed around Liverpool city centre's tourist sites and I remember being struck by little more than how many cathedrals there were. As was often the case with my mum's spontaneous days out, it all ended with a frantic rush to catch the last train home back to the place where I've spent my entire life right up until now.

My mum came from a good, church-going background. Unlike many of the families on the Meadows estate, ours had no history of criminality stretching back through the generations. My family were what you might call respectable working class. They believed in God and education. On paper, that might seem like a blessing. But in practice it would become something of a curse.

My mum was incredibly generous and warm-hearted. She couldn't pass a homeless person without offering to help. She also ran her own Sunday school. I went regularly and even got confirmed there. Maybe those early experiences laid the foundations for my later redemption.

Through my mum's connection with a local church, she managed to get me a place in a primary school that was technically outside the catchment area of where we lived. The school was in an area called Wilford, which is on the opposite side of the River Trent. Here the demographic couldn't have been more different to the toughness of The Meadows.

Wilford had a more gentile, village feel – albeit that it's quite close to Nottingham city centre. Most people owned their own homes and many of these properties were expensive; there were some nice cars sitting on the driveways. Because of the church connection, and the fact that I'd gone to pre-school there for a few years, I was admitted to the primary school.

I only have good memories of the place. I lived for the moment and for each day. I felt completely secure in myself and in my relationships with others. I had no problem asking teachers questions in the classroom and I was keen to learn. On a wider level, all the pupils got along well and I became friendly with some of the kids from the Wilford area, including a couple whose parents were teachers at school – I still know them today.

In the holidays I'd be allowed to go on bike rides over to where these friends lived. I think my mum felt that being in the Wilford area, with these kinds of friends, was good for me. And it probably was. It felt like there was no spotlight shining on me and, equally significantly, I never felt the need to question myself, even though we certainly still got up to mischief: pinching sweets from shops and robbing car dust caps for our bikes.

If going to school and interacting with kids outside of The Meadows caused any issues when I went back home, I wasn't aware of it then. I don't recall ever feeling resentful or jealous of these friends for anything they had that I didn't.

I suppose that even though we lived in The Meadows we were probably relatively well off compared to some of our neighbours. Mum ran a child-minding business from home. She also had a mortgage, which was relatively unusual in our neighbourhood.

So while you could never say that we were well off per se, we were by no means the worst. The margins we're talking about were small ones, though. It wasn't a flash existence. Perhaps my brother and I had one extra pair of trainers or a couple of extra tracksuits relative to the average kids. While we did go on an occasional holiday as a family, I later found out that my mum had taken out seven credit cards to fund such things.

I can't fault my mum in any way though. While she probably wasn't great at managing money and lived beyond her means most of the time, she did it all with the aim of giving Sam and I as happy and full a childhood as she possibly could.

No amount of credit-card-funded living could hide the fact that we were still a run-of-the-mill single-parent family living on a deprived council estate, however. And when I transitioned to secondary school, I really started to feel the burden of this family dynamic.

On reflection, the most significant tipping point in my entire life came at this transition point between primary and secondary school. As I approached the age of 12 or 13, my dad's absence started to feel like a dense cloud hanging over me.

My parents had divorced when I was just seven, and my dad moved back to his local area of Partington, near Manchester. I didn't see him again until my tenth birthday – and then again when I was fourteen on our way to watch an England game at Old Trafford. It wasn't until I turned sixteen that I would go up to see him more sporadically. In his words, 'You didn't want to be here; you were polite but very quiet and withdrawn. But after that first visit you did start to come up a bit more often.' Anyway, I don't really remember much about him from my early life. One of the few things I do remember is playing football with him and being taken to a Nottingham Forest game for one of my birthday parties. Besides that, there were trips to the seaside, American Adventure and football training.

I also know his relationship with my mum was volatile at times. There was alcohol involved – on both sides. They clearly were not happy together.

After he left, much as he tried to maintain a relationship with my brother and me – initially through supervised visits at contact centres. I remember these being quite traumatic days with my mum, who would bail out of visits a the last minute. The reality was that cards and money at birthdays and Christmas was all there was in terms of contact from my dad.

For a few years, I suppose this was enough. A young boy has little awareness of much beyond basic realities and I suppose I was getting what I needed from my primary school life and summer camps anyway.

However, when I began that shift into youth from childhood, I started becoming aware of some of the things I didn't have. These weren't tangible things. As much as I would have liked simply to be with my dad – to go to a football match or for him to watch me taking part in school activities – it was the subtle, emotional input that I was missing, that only a male role model could offer. I wasn't the only one. Many of my friends at that time didn't have a dad in their lives either.

What was also unique and perhaps significant is the specific school culture I went into in year seven. This particular school had been essentially mothballed a few years earlier under a different name. It had had all kinds of historical disciplinary problems; the building itself had fallen into disrepair and needed a major overhaul.

By the time I reached secondary school age, it had only recently been reopened and with very limited pupil numbers, and as an odd consequence of that there was only one older year group above me.

At the time, my mum genuinely thought that a school with fewer pupils would be good for me. I've never really thought about how that all played out until recently, but with hindsight now I think it made for a situation whereby we never had those much older kids to look up to from year seven onwards. Equally, there was nobody older to keep us in line at a time when we were most likely to be testing boundaries.

I'll never know whether the more general feelings of confusion about my emotional needs arrived as a coincidence of my moving to the Emmanuel Secondary School or because of it. Either way, it didn't matter. From the age of 12, having been flung into a new and intimidating teenage world with only a few of the kids I'd been around previously, my outlook changed completely

Almost overnight, I started feeling a lot less confident in myself, and more anxious about how others viewed me. I felt the harsh glow of the peer-group spotlight at school and in parallel I'd go home and put myself under a microscope of my own, worrying about all the changes that teenage life can bring.

Of course, I had no answers. I certainly had no idea who I really was or where I fitted in. Not many teenagers are equipped to solve these kinds of life issues. Instead, we just react on impulse to how we feel, and have little control over it.

Inside, I was unsure of myself, my place in life – even what kinds of people I should be being friendly with. It was constant inner turmoil, but you'd never have known to look at me because my façade was telling the world that I was this carefree, confident and happy lad.

Sadly, living behind a façade can only carry someone – far less a confused teenager – so far. The truth is that it's totally counterproductive. The problems just manifest. And without a single older male role model to share my worries with, look up to or feel guilty about letting down, it was perhaps unavoidable that my life, much as with many other kids like me, went in the direction it did.

Within the school, there was probably a fifty-fifty split of kids from decent backgrounds outside The Meadows and those from troubled families within it. It was at this point that I felt that I needed to identify with somebody or something – and I chose to seek approval from the latter group.

Looking back, there was an obvious reason why I chose this demographic, and it essentially came down to geographical convenience in the sense that, rather than having to get on a bus after school to go home to a different area, and a better life, I just had to walk home with the kids from the neighbourhood where I lived. It made total sense that these troubled kids became my peer group. But it was a decision that would alter the course of my life.

And the changes came fast. Having been a good learner at primary school, I started playing up in class to impress these new friends – and bear in mind that these were kids who were probably kicking off in class at primary school, throwing tables and chairs at each other as a matter of course. This was behaviour that was unheard of where I went to primary school.

Before long, their attitudes were rubbing off on me and sticking. I went from having a good relationship with teachers and a respect for authority, to being seen as a bit of a disruptive troublemaker. Pretty soon my stock responses to teachers' questions became, 'I don't know', 'I'm not bothered.'

I liked how this new role made me feel (I was certainly getting affirmation from my peers which temporarily boosted my flagging self-esteem), but my relationship with my mum soon became more toxic around this transition point – simply because she was simultaneously trying to do the job of both parents. I remember feeling so scared the first time the school told me they were going to ring my mum about my behaviour.

And from there it was a fast downward spiral. The worse I felt and the more my schoolwork suffered as a result, the more she tried to rein me in and the harder I rebelled against her.

Ironically, while I was increasingly AWOL during those first two years at secondary school, my poor, frantic mum was never out of the school office.

Phone calls from the school about my behaviour were a daily event. I feel so guilty about this now that my mum is no longer here. At the time, she still saw me as the good learner I'd been at primary school and she was desperate to reinforce the belief that I couldn't have just become a bad kid overnight. As she pushed and pushed for reasons why I was suddenly so hard to manage at school, it got to the point where the only option was to have me psychologically assessed. I guess the school had run out of ideas as to how to control me.

I should say – and this seems so strange in retrospect – that neither my mum nor I ever sat in on these consultations that talked about me, how to support me or to manage my behaviour. At no point was I involved in the decisions about any potential solutions. In the end, they arrived at the conclusion that I had a combination of ADHD, dyslexia and a condition that put me somewhere on the autism spectrum. Thereafter, I was given no support in terms of helping me understand the implications of these diagnoses.

What all this meant for us was that my mum was able to claim some disability allowance on my behalf. That was a positive, I suppose. But for me these diagnoses were the worst thing that could have happened at that time. Instead of clarifying anything in my mind, they made me give up. Instead of being something to overcome, these conditions – which a group of experts had arbitrarily decided I had – just gave me licence to do even less in school. We'd be sitting in an English lesson, and I'd just say, 'Well, I've got dyslexia, so fuck it. I'm not even going to try.' I'd been given an excuse that I could legitimately hide behind.

What didn't help in any way were the methods the school used to punish and control kids like me. We had a room that was simply called 'isolation', and it did exactly what was written on the tin: you were left in a room alone with a senior teacher while they did paperwork. You just had to sit there in silence – in social isolation.

Similarly, people like me were often put in lower sets of classes. All that made me feel was that even the teachers were acknowledging I didn't need to try. Nobody was talking to me in a way that was solution-focused. It was simply a case of them managing difficult behaviour while investing as few resources as possible in doing so. That made me more resentful and rebellious.

Equally, via these diagnoses, my mum had been given something that she could use to explain to other people why I was like I was.

I remember on one occasion being at a nearby farm where they had pedal go-karts. I was flying around this track with my cousin.

Granted, I was going way too fast and there was another kid on the track going much slower. As I went around a corner, I flipped my kart and went flying out of it in front of this other kid, who wasn't hurt at all. Nevertheless, this kid's mum was screaming at me, and in return my mum was yelling back at her, saying words to the effect of: 'He has autism! He has autism!'

Really all she needed to say was, 'Slow down, Jacob. Be more careful.'

But instead, in that moment, it felt like she was shaming me. Looking back, it wasn't her fault. She was just upset by the embarrassment and simply didn't have the right information to know how to handle a situation like that – nobody really did.

So, as much as these diagnoses changed how I lived my life, they also fundamentally changed how my mum parented me. As my focus moved away from English and Maths lessons towards what was going on in friends' houses and on the estate generally, my mum desperately tried to reel me in. Whenever I'd be at this particular friend's place, whose only present parent was his dad, she'd make a point of coming around to look for me.

This dad's attitude was that he'd rather we were skiving off school and in his house, than out causing trouble somewhere else. Clearly he'd given up trying, but at least he could keep an eye on us.

My mum didn't share his relaxed outlook, however. She kept trying to exert parental influence when it was clear I wanted none of it. She'd forever be banging on the door and shouting: 'Jacob? Are you there? What are you doing?' It was as if she was trying to shame me in front of my friends.

So, this slow degeneration occurred after my diagnoses – from being given detentions all the time and being forced to report to the head teacher every day with a report card signed by every other teacher, to being followed around the school to make sure I was in class. Every day was degrading and demoralising. Eventually I started thinking that it was a lot easier to just not go to school at all.

Around the same time, because we were increasingly skiving school as a group, my friends and I inevitably experimented with drinking for the first time, which in turn led to low-level criminality along the lines of vandalism, fire-raising, trespassing and window-smashing – all for no reason other than we were bored and we could.

Conveniently for us disassociated youths, they had started making bus shelters out of glass, so they all got broken. Any new-builds in the area were fair game for being broken into and vandalised. Other days we'd go to one of the bridges over the River Trent and throw rocks at boats.

I'm not proud of any of this behaviour and it in no way justifies any of it when I say that vodka, in combination with being with a 'team', made me feel like I could do anything. But I did get such a huge buzz and temporary relief from my problems. In these moments I felt so alive – with no shit given for anything else.

Part of me thinks that if we'd kept it at drinking without the aggression that came with it, things would have worked out okay. The other part knows that half of all homicide victims have been drinking alcohol, in addition to half of the perpetrators.

Either way, at the time we didn't stop – we were continually egging each other on from one level to the next. Our horizons were forever being broadened.

Chapter Two

Gang Land

Unsurprisingly, The Meadows that I knew in my younger years had morphed into a completely different entity by the time I hit the age of 14. In reality, it hadn't changed much, but it was my perception of it that had.

When you're 9 years old, you don't know that the kids circling endlessly around the shopping parade wearing hoodies are actually drug dealers. You have no idea that by crossing one street into another you're violating drug territory.

As a kid, you just see a place on a childish level: a betting shop, a street – a kid on a pushbike. As a young teenager, it's as if a veil has been drawn back. Places and people become clear for what they are, and the threats and the dangers become real. And on The Meadows, these dangers truly were very present and real. I remember witnessing a drive-by shooting one night on my way home from my aunty's house. I also remember lying under my covers listening as people robbed gardens near my house.

I know that some people think gang culture is a game and the stuff of overblown television dramas. The reality is that it's worse than that and it's taken very seriously on both sides of the dividing line. Codes of honour existed; each side even wore distinctive blue or red colours for a while. Territories were clearly defined. Disputes, and there are many, were resolved with unglamorous violence. People got badly hurt, sometimes killed if caught 'slippin'. Other people went to jail. Gang violence was and still is real in the most mundane way – and a single estate in Nottingham is just the tip of the iceberg for this country.

The Meadows was named after an area of meadow farmland that was susceptible to being flooded by the nearby River Trent. The neighbourhood today has with a fair amount of notoriety attached to it. Largely built in the Victorian era to house labourers who were working on the Midland railway line, the estate as we know it now is split into two distinct parts: the Old Meadows, which is comprised of terraced houses of the Victorian style, and the New Meadows, built in the 1970s – an architecturally brutalist layout of council houses separated by unbounded open spaces and connected by multiple alleyways, underpasses and feeder roads designed to keep pedestrians and traffic apart according to the Radburn planning model that emerged post-slum clearance.

In theory, this concept made total sense. It was designed to create an open-feeling, 'green' living environment, and from a purely aesthetic standpoint it did.

But in practice, combined with escalating poverty and gang culture in the area, its layout was a weakness in that it facilitated petty crime, simply because the houses were close together, overlooking each other and with indistinct exterior boundaries.

Furthermore, its complex series of connecting alleyways merely aided escape for those who cared to learn the intricacies. 'Local knowledge' was a vital skill for the aspiring criminal to acquire. Although there were cameras everywhere, it was possible to get from one end of The Meadows to another using almost exclusively tunnels and narrow alleys. At times it felt like a multi-level video game.

The focus of everything is still the Meadows Bridgeway Centre – an unattractive canyon of a thoroughfare with shops either side and flats above. This is where crime most often happened and still happens today. Someone was tragically shot there not so long ago. The scenes that have occurred on this strip over the years could easily inspire a spin-off of *Shameless*.

On one corner stands a pub – The Poet's Corner – and outside a row of beleaguered alcoholics or drug addicts is often assembled, waiting for a dealer to appear out of the woodwork. There is no conversation – in stark contrast to the kind of 'ay-up me duck!' greetings that you'd hear from down-to-earth folk.

Then there's Arkwright Walk – the most notorious street on the estate and home to the older, more established gang members. As my nan used to remind me, it was once a thriving thoroughfare linking Nottingham city centre to Trent Bridge, with shops along its route and open to buses. However, as local businesses closed on the back of out-of-town retail park development, the council blocked off the road to all vehicles, leaving behind a pedestrianised hotbed for petty crime.

Arkwright Walk was just a three-minute walk from my house on Bathley Street, and I used to go up there to stay at a friend's right at the top of the road. Because we weren't allowed out, we'd often just sit at his bedroom window being fascinated by all the lads out there, clearly up to no good.

At the other end of The Meadows altogether, in the newer council estate part, there's another thoroughfare running through the middle called Bosworth Walk – a similarly notorious hotbed for crime and an area that was home to a number of my friends. These are the two main territories, and outsiders were safe in neither.

As I moved through my teenage years, I started becoming more aware of the nuances of gang rivalry that existed between these two parts of the estate. The conflict, as far as I understood it, was motivated by a couple of different conditions.

First, there was and still is a general lack of opportunity, coupled with poverty. When people simply have no means of advancing their lives, crime becomes the only 'safe' method of survival. It's the path of least resistance – especially when so many in one area feel the same way and there is a family history of arrest and imprisonment.

What happens then is that each successive generation becomes ingrained with the idea that the 'straight' life offers them nothing, and that authority is to be challenged. Whether they have any aspirations of their own or not, it's hard for young people on estates like The Meadows to push back against this pervasive, negative and often inherited worldview. Over a period of a few generations, criminality becomes endemic among the population. The cycle is almost impossible to break.

Second, and this is a product of the first, drugs are a big factor – simply because they are one of the few ways available to make money when you have none. Inevitably, the sale of these drugs – weed, cocaine, crack and heroin being the perennial mainstays – becomes a source of huge conflict, and at the same time, it's an entirely territorial enterprise.

Weed is at the bottom end of the drug scale and it's relatively low value. Heroin and crack on the other hand command the highest value and therefore are liable to be the most common source of conflict between rivals that are selling.

Dealers have their designated patches. Violation of these patches leads to conflict. Conflict leads to retaliation, and so it goes on to the point that an estate like The Meadows is in a constant state of gang-related rivalry – often perpetuated by a number of historically criminal families that might have two or three generations still living on the estate. The older ones groom and encourage the younger ones who find themselves hanging around on these streets.

Where I was very different from most was that my family had absolutely no legacy of criminality whatsoever. As I said, my mum came from a good church-going family and my dad was from a different part of the country. To that extent, I was a complete outsider, and that position was something of a double-edged sword.

On one level, I could fly totally under the radar. Nobody really knew who I was, who my dad was or who my uncle was, or whoever. They had no point of reference for my past family indiscretions, and there weren't any to find anyway.

On the flipside, because The Meadows is composed of so many 'known' multi-generational families, if someone could say 'such and such is my uncle' or 'so and so is my cousin' when in a tight spot, often they'd get a free pass and wouldn't be challenged. But not having any kind of reputation for criminality in my family put me in a weak position from a credibility perspective when I started turning up, trying to act like the big man, at some of my friends' houses.

'You've lived here all your life, you say? We've never seen you around …' the adult males would say, eyes narrowed to slits.

I'd just nod.

And there were the loudmouth brats with pumped-up egos, fuelled by their family ties and their need to reinforce this perceived dominance.

'Where you from?' 'Who's your dad? We don't fucking know you.'

I could tell that my lack of history made them deeply suspicious. Because of that I felt that I had to go a step further than most of the people in my peer group just to prove myself, though I'm not sure my friends would have seen it that way.

In my mind I had to walk taller, talk tougher, drink more vodka and, ultimately, fight harder to demonstrate that my lack of hard-man heritage was by no means a hindrance to my being part of this diverse group of disenfranchised youths, many of whom were mixed race or black (there were many African-Caribbean families living in The Meadows) and many of whom had a similarly cynical view of what life could possibly offer them.

Most of our dialogue around this time was centred on who was the toughest – a uniquely teenage-male kind of subject matter. No kidding, we'd have daily conversations about who would be in the top three hardest or who we'd like to see fight each other. If a new person turned up at school or in the neighbourhood, our first collective thought would be: 'What area are they from?' And the second would be: 'How fucking hard are they and what have they done in the past to prove it?'

Aggression, and its potential applications in our lives, was a large part of what we talked about as 15-year-olds. Everything was about who could outdo the other or go furthest in terms of their imagined violence – as opposed to actual acts of violence against other people, which would come later.

At no point did any of us actually voice in specific terms what it was about life that made us feel so hopeless and angry. It wasn't as if we ever sat around in a bedroom or talked on the way to school – on the very few occasions we went – about exactly how we felt and why. For some reason you just didn't do that – and especially boys.

What was obvious though, albeit unsaid, was that we all shared a vague sense of not really belonging anywhere and that the system was set up to ensure that we'd fail.

It was a nihilistic worldview, and the fact that many of my friends came from families with a history of crime – where one or more of their parents was either in or had been in prison, didn't help anyone. After all, whenever someone was released from prison, the first thing they did was reinforce to their community how prison was something to be proud of and how the system – and life in general – was geared against people like them. None of my friends knew of any success stories, and there was no one on the estate who could offer them a more positive outlook, other than a few footballers, the odd rapper and a bunch of flashy dealers.

But I was subject to none of these conditions. Other than this negative peer group and the bad decisions I had made because of my involvement with them, I had no real reason to be hating life like I was. Whereas these friends had been feeling that way because of their shared experiences throughout primary school, it was all relatively new to me.

Despite this – with my own desperate need for affirmation fuelling me, and any vague notions of getting an education far behind me – I found myself being drawn deeper into The Meadows' criminal subculture. If you were being cynical, I suppose you could say that the people I was hanging around with were subtly grooming me, perhaps without even knowing it.

Gradually I was growing into the culture, developing the beginnings of a gang mentality whereby I felt like I really belonged in the neighbourhood that my mum had tried so hard to shield me from for the first part of my life.

By the time I turned fifteen and a half, I'd hit what many would see as a roadblock. I'd been kicked out of school with no qual-ifications; I had absolutely no direction in life. While she hadn't physically booted me out of the house, my mum had pretty much given up on trying to get me to do anything worthwhile. She didn't approve of the way I was living but was becoming increasingly resigned to it.

The truth is that I liked this position of inertia. I didn't want a direction in life. I didn't want to try something new or get up every morning to go to work or college. Instead, I wanted to keep my no-responsibility going as long as possible. I wanted to do absolutely nothing.

So I spent most days just sitting at friends' houses playing PlayStation, smoking weed and listening to British rap, niche and grime. That was an average day.

It was natural, I suppose, that we were listening to this kind of music, for all the reasons you'd expect, and I suspect many people of my age would be happy to admit that it was a soundtrack to their youth too. After all, it was loud, confrontational, anti-authority – all in keeping with our worldview.

Looking back, it motivated us too – not to do something, but to fight the system by not doing something. That was the appeal for me. I liked American music too. While it seemed miles from Nottingham and less culturally relevant, the general dissatisfaction spoke to me somehow and I could relate it to my own experiences.

I reckon far fewer lads of my age are willing to acknowledge that they also watched a Japanese manga series called *Naruto*, but quite a lot of my mates did so obsessively – to the extent that I'm not ashamed to admit that later, while I was in prison, I thought nothing of contacting my friends on a Sunday morning, when they were probably all hungover, just to find out what happened in that week's episode.

For our group of friends, it was this once-weekly dose of pure escapism that we got into during our mid-teens and stayed with thereafter. On paper, its whimsical, philosophical storylines were completely at odds with the tough-guy image we wanted to portray, but it was so well written, blending beautiful characterisations with relatable life lessons, that we just couldn't resist it. I'm sure I wouldn't be exaggerating if I said that it probably gave a lot of young men their first and only sense of any kind of moral compass. For me, especially in combination with weed, *Naruto* had such a calming effect that it was the perfect counterbalance to the dysfunctional chaos of our lives.

Honestly, I look back on these times with a kind of twisted fondness. During the days, I wasn't getting into too much trouble; I was keeping a low profile and everything was cool. I wasn't bothering anyone – and not much was bothering me. But it didn't take long for me to realise that even doing nothing costs something – particularly when you're into getting on it, playing consoles and smoking weed.

Up until that point, I should say that my relationship with alcohol had probably been like that of most other teenagers. Because you don't have much money and even less tolerance, you start by drinking cheap vodka neat from the bottle in the local park and then blacking out.

Later, you wake up semi-clothed and disorientated on the sofa in some random friend's house and notice that you've been sick on your shoes on the way to the toilet. You then spend the rest of the day recovering, watching TV and eventually hearing from your friends about some of the stupid things you said or did the previous night. Maybe you're horrified to learn that you set fire to the bin in the park before you passed out. It's all very mundane and predictable, but smoking weed and getting on it also costs money.

So, what do you do?

Well, when you're 15 and living on a housing estate and you don't want to work but still want to buy drugs and alcohol, one of the only ways of generating income is by selling drugs – and they're not exactly hard to find in a place like The Meadows. Other lads went creeping into people's homes and businesses to burgle them. Personally, given how hard my mum had to work for the possessions we had, that concept never sat that well with me.

But how do you even start with a drug enterprise?

Well, I just decided to buy half an ounce of weed off a guy on the estate to see how far it could take me.

I started selling first to my friends. Relatively speaking, selling cannabis is not what you'd call a profitable enterprise – and really it didn't need to be. When you're still living at home and not being asked to pay rent, the hundred quid that you could make off selling an ounce of weed represented a lot when you could get a bottle of vodka for less than a tenner.

Apart from that, it wasn't as if I spent much other than on food, and, occasionally, clothes. I had it all sorted, I thought. But, as chilled as these days were, the nights, and specifically weekend nights, were anything but.

It's important to say at this point that most young people who get involved in gang activities do so not because they particularly want to be part of a gang, but more because it's the easiest thing to do at that time.

Granted, there are and always will be individuals whose lives revolve solely around gang-related activities – the hardliners, the lifers. These people will become habitual criminals, and will probably spend their twenties, thirties and forties entering and exiting prison on a constant, depressing loop. But I was never one of those people. I was someone who operated on the fringes, fraternising with a combination of others – a few of whom had serious gang aspirations, but most of whom were in a similar situation to me in that they quite frankly had nothing better to do.

This might sound a bit flippant, but looking back on it all now, I had one foot in gang culture and one foot out from the beginning. I wasn't dedicating my life to it by any means; I was just doing it for laughs at the weekend, getting drunk, getting into fights and so on. Some of my friends were a lot more involved though, and this is where it got a little complicated for me.

Coincidentally, when I was around 16, there was a subtle change in the gang culture in The Meadows, and it seemed to happen quite quickly from my perspective.

Initially, the rivalry was solely between gangs from different parts of the city. For a while, it was probably as though the Bloods and the Crips rivalry from 1960s Los Angeles was being re-enacted here in Nottingham. Gang members from The Meadows wore blue; their St Ann's (an area in the north-east of the city) rivals wore red and Radford wore black.

Some of the lads I was hanging about with would actively seek out trouble with rival gangs. They would pile into a car and drive to another part of the city to cause harm. Of course this exercise carried with it a new set of risks – not least because by this time many more people were carrying knives.

There's been a lot of conversation about knife crime in recent years and rightly so – it's a huge problem that blights almost every urban centre in the country – far more so than it was back in my street-fighting days. People always seem to want to complicate and intellectualise it, and that, to me at least, has always been a little puzzling.

As far as I saw it (I witnessed the rise of knife culture), the reason for the appearance of knives on our streets is no more complicated than armies in history upgrading from one kind of weapon to another. In almost every situation, humans select a weapon because whatever they have at their disposal is no longer deemed sufficient relative to who or what they're up against.

Jacob Dunne

This rethink was forced on The Meadows in the mid-2000s, when young lads from one part of the estate went to another to cause trouble, only to be confronted not only by angry young lads, but also by grizzled 30-year-old men – hardened criminals, many of whom had probably recently been in jail a few times.

In that kind of a situation, no matter how hard you think you are, you're going to lose. So, what are you going to do? You're going to even the playing field – and you're going to do it as cheaply as possible. A knife fits that bill on every level, and they can be bought anywhere by anyone, or just nicked from the nearest kitchen drawer.

Before too long, knives were everywhere. I carried one now and again; all my friends carried too. Not just that, everyone in every other neighbourhood had one also. It became a total free-for-all, with people getting stabbed all over the place, for all manner of things – mostly related to territory, respect and egos. Knives completely changed the landscape.

Friends of mine would drive to other areas to harm people or to 'catch someone slippin'' – a gang slang expression used for when someone gets caught unawares by rival gang members.

'I caught you slippin',' you'd say – which is to imply that that person wasn't ready, isn't safe anywhere and needs to watch their own back 24/7.

This kind of activity would happen all the time, and it worked both ways. Believe me, I've been chased around the estate late at night more than once by cars full of people from other areas. I had a few close shaves, and I've seen people that got caught slippin' get badly hurt. Luck, and the fact that I had yet to make too many enemies, was the only thing that prevented something similar happening to me.

Then something else was added to the mix. Gang rivalry started escalating within each area like The Meadows itself. Arkwright and Bosworth residents on the estate would be at each other's throats. Instead of having to drive to another part of town to commit violence, suddenly there was confrontation to be had right on your own doorstep. That changed everything – and made The Meadows a much more dangerous place.

But much as I wasn't invested in gang activity to anything like the same extent as some of my friends, there was a nuance to all of this that impacted on me. While I was definitely more interested in going on nights out to pubs and getting into fights, I'd ultimately end up getting drawn into gang-related conflict, simply because of who my friends were.

So, if any of my friends who had this reputation were ever seen by a rival gang on a (relatively) innocent night out with me, I'd always end up having to fight to defend my friends, even though I didn't personally subscribe to the gang ideology or have any issues with the person I ended up fighting.

Some people would assume that being on the periphery of a gang is easier, but for me, as long as I wanted to go on nights out, it was always going to be a very difficult situation for me to juggle – and the most bizarre part is that I was hiding as much of this information as I possibly could from my mum.

As I turned 17, however, it wouldn't be long before The Meadows lost its appeal and girls and the city centre beckoned.

Chapter Three

The Punch

There came a point, and I felt and acknowledged it at the time, where my confidence and self-esteem improved in direct relation to the number of crimes I committed. As counterintuitive as it might sound, bad things really did equal good feelings. And the reason for this was that, with every criminal act completed – drug deal done, street brawl won, weekend session completed, police pursuit averted, and, when caught, every 'no comment' interview – I got more and more acceptance from my peer group.

The more I belonged, the more I grew as a person and started believing my own hype. Dickheads that used to think they could push me about, just because they wanted to, would start thinking twice and I could sense them doing it. My God, that felt good.

'Alright Jacob,' I used to think to myself, 'you really are the big man now.'

And the funny thing is: even if I knew that this life would definitely catch up with me, I still craved more.

Nottingham city centre was the uncharted frontier. As violent and crime-ridden and entertaining as The Meadows undoubtedly was, it had become strangely familiar – almost 'safe'.

Yes, there were some right nutters at the top of Bosworth who we'd never mess with. Certainly, there were some of the St Ann's crew that we wouldn't want to be caught slippin' by on a Friday night. But I remember feeling a sense that The Meadows was a known quantity and that even more excitement lay beyond it.

The city centre was a completely different proposition. And the aspect that made it so attractive was that, unlike other major cities where you might need to get on a bus to travel to and from the centre, Nottingham city centre was just a 20-minute walk across the river. It was piss-easy getting to and from home. We could come and go as we pleased, at any time of day and night. And we did.

Initially it was all quite innocent. There were some girls from our school around at that time and a lot of what we were doing was just bravado among our group and these girls – normal territory for 17- and 18-year-olds. In the brief moments when we were sober, our conversations were always the same: who was making the most money selling drugs, which criminal family was hardest and who was in jail for what. We talked about life like someone else might discuss *EastEnders*, except we were actually living it.

By the time we were off our heads, everything became a blur as the substances merely lit the touchpaper to ignite the inner rage we all shared and that we had no idea how to channel, other than by indulging in increasingly antisocial acts of violence and machismo.

The toughest thing to admit about all of this is that, as many beers as we had or lines of coke we snorted, none of those highs could even touch how I felt when I saw the sheer admiration on my friends' faces when I fought alongside them, roaring, stripped to the waist in the street, to defend their honour as if we were in *Game of Thrones*.

For me, the look in their eyes was the ultimate high that ranked alongside pulling a fit girl. It was intoxicating and a little frightening at the same time, because I didn't know how far it might push me as more and more of my associates started going to prison.

I can say without hesitation that, when you're engaged in criminality, even on a low level, there comes a moment where you subconsciously seek out 'heavier' people to interact with. While you're still technically in your group of friends and loyal to them as a collective, there is definitely a temptation to extend your network into criminal elements outside your group. And in Nottingham city centre, there's no shortage of them. When your tongue loosens late at night, your paths will collide.

As a result of this curiosity, it wasn't long before, having been an absolute criminal nobody on my own estate, I found myself doing this strange kind of networking with a variety of different types of criminal elements, from organised crime types doing God-knows-what, to higher-level drug dealers.

Instead of being intimidated I felt the opposite. Somehow, I always seemed to find a way to do just enough in various situations, and to strike just the right note of credibility with these new connections, to keep myself alive in situations that under normal circumstances would be chronically dangerous. Instead of feeling any sense that the roof of my world was about to cave in, there was this strange sensation of safety and belonging within serious criminality instead.

Some of the situations I got myself into, you wouldn't believe. Drink and drugs will make you forget whole days, believe me. A night out could easily turn into a week-long bender. And I'd often find myself thinking, 'Who the fuck did I meet on day three of all that and what did I say to them?'

I'd answer phone calls, staring at the grimy, cracked and barely decipherable phone screen held together by tape, in a mixture of fear and disbelief, thinking: 'How the fuck have I got this person's name and number in my phone? And what have I talked my way into?'

I remember one morning when this well-known hot-head knocked on the door of our house. He was on his own bender, and he had not only remembered that I'd been on a session with him sometime in the past, but also where I fucking lived.

'I've got to lay down somewhere mate,' he said. 'I don't have anywhere to go.'

'I've got bloody work in half an hour ...' I told him, desperately searching for a way to get out of the situation without him going crazy on me.

But he barged in anyway, and headed for the sofa.

'Mate, please, you've got to get the fuck out,' I told him, struggling to reconcile these two elements of my life: the total mundanity of my home, and the absolute chaos of the 'me' I was when I went out at night getting on a session.

Events like that were common, and I never knew when they were going to happen. Gradually I started accumulating this collection of criminal contacts and the weirdest part of it all was that, on hearing my story and seeing me as increasingly legit, they'd start creating narratives – narratives that were completely false – to endear themselves to me!

'I knew your mum,' someone would say.

'My dad said he went to school with your dad ...' another might claim.

Neither of these statements was true, especially the latter, but in their minds, I suppose it made us more alike and my credibility only grew as a result.

Even at this point, despite the increasingly shady connections I was making, my main motivation was still to get on it – being under the influence of drugs and alcohol – as often as possible. And that's what happened. I chased parties more, didn't ever want to be at home other than if injured or recovering, and only wanted to be around people who thought the same way as I did.

What I found was that there was no shortage of people who wanted the same thing. Naturally I gravitated towards them and, as a result, any relationships I had with friends who were doing A-Levels or were thinking about going to university just faded away.

Looking back on this period now, nothing I was doing was balanced. Just like anything in life, if you do too much of something, other areas of your life suffer.

In my case, I was doing so much drinking and taking so many drugs that I lost track of any of the other responsibilities I needed to grow up.

You don't realise this at the time, of course, because you're too deep in what you're doing. It's only later when you look back that you realise that you've lost your relationship with your family and have failed to hold down any kind of responsibility whatsoever in terms of employment or further education. Before you know it, you are isolated from everything other than a destructive lifestyle and the people within it.

Anything I did on the side was done solely to fund my evening drinking and drugs activities. At one point I was helping Travellers collect scrap metal during the daytime and taking stuff that I shouldn't have taken. Any bits of metal I found lying around in Nottingham, no matter who owned it, just got thrown in the back of a van without a thought or care. The job was a means to an end. Scrap metal meant more alcohol and maybe a 're-load' – a slang term used for a restocking of drugs.

Later I also worked at the Boots distribution centre – where pretty much every working-class person in the area has put in a few shifts at some point in their life.

Unlike the scrap metal collecting job, there was just too much structure at Boots. I had to show up at a certain time – and on my first day I was late because I stayed up all night with my mates trying to complete a console game. People, bosses, told me what to do and when. I lasted about three weeks before quitting and thinking, 'Fuck this.'

Throughout all of this, given that I was still living at home, my mum was fighting an increasingly losing battle to the extent that she was barely fighting at all. If she ever did offer any opinions about what I should have been doing with my life, I was belligerent and unreceptive.

In truth, because of the hours I kept and my chaotic state of mind, there were rarely any moments of civility in which any normal conversations could happen anyway. It wasn't like we had family dinners together when everyone was at home. And the rest of the time I just wouldn't be at home at all. I'd simply be using her house as a place to recover, coming in and out as I pleased and with no regard for anyone else.

I took total advantage of my mum's unconditional love, basically. By the age of 18, I knew exactly what I could and could not get away with. As strict as she was in her house in the sense that I was never allowed to bring friends around, I don't think she ever seriously wanted to kick me out – surely she must have considered it every now and again – even though she must have known I was constantly in trouble.

I suppose in her mind she must have decided that to do so would only push me further down the negative path I was on, and she was probably right. Being booted out of my family home wouldn't have been the kind of wake-up call I needed to re-evaluate my life. The truth is, I didn't want to re-evaluate my life. I just wanted to continue doing what I was doing for as long as I possibly could.

Ego, a desire to impress my mates and, naturally, a cocktail of drugs and alcohol were the forces that combined to mean that fights were a regular part of life on nights out in the city centre.

Because I was still experimenting with my tolerance for drugs and alcohol, I'd be totally blanking out most nights. I wouldn't even remember being in a fight until somebody reminded me the next day.

Looking back, this place of chemically induced ignorance was a very dangerous place to be. We'd be sitting in someone's house, totally hung-over, saying stuff like, 'Mate, what even happened last night?' or 'How the fuck did we get home?'

We simply didn't know anything until one of us triggered a memory that allowed us to assemble a hazy picture of the previous night's events. Then we'd recall just basic fragments of information, like who got in a fight with whom and where, who pulled a girl and that we'd ran home being chased by the police through alleyways. These were the only details that mattered.

Police chases were common in those days. On the few nights when I held it together enough to recall what happened, I found myself running down lanes and hiding behind parked cars and wheelie bins while the police drove up and down our road looking for me.

On one occasion, a police car actually mounted the pavement in an attempt to corner me. I don't remember being scared. I felt more like I was in an exciting action movie or a video game.

I think probably the reason I wasn't afraid was because, on the few instances when I was actually arrested, nothing much happened anyway. I'd just get questioned, tell the police nothing, they'd have no evidence to charge me with an actual crime – and then, after a night in a holding cell at the notorious Bridewell Police Station, they'd release me the next day and I'd just walk back home.

It was all a bit pointless really and certainly no deterrent. Whenever anyone said, 'Yeah, I just spent a night in Bridewell', it was considered both a bit of a joke and a badge of honour.

People have often asked me whether at any point on this destructive trajectory I ever paused to consider the many possible bad outcomes that could have arisen. And the answer is that, yes, I did consider some of the awful things that could potentially occur. After all, I had witnessed lots of them.

But honestly, I was so far gone that any threat of calamity didn't scare me; it excited me more than anything else – which isn't an easy admission to make given how things played out.

The reality of the matter is that the culture I was embroiled in was completely drama-orientated: who took things the furthest / drank the most / was the hardest in a particular street-fight and so forth. Furthermore, all these acts of vandalism or violence soon became normalised to the extent that I think I was desensitised to the possibility of life completely spiralling out of control.

I needed drama in my 19-year-old life, simply because the alternative was to become a normal person living a regular nine-to-five, taxpaying, legal life – and that was an idea that didn't attract me at all.

In truth, normal life scared me because I didn't believe I was capable of doing well in that environment. The way I saw it, I had tried the Boots factory, selling scrap metal and selling weed for a bit of money.

The first two didn't work out, because I didn't want them to work out. And the only good aspects about selling weed were that it kept me around my mates and actually stopped us getting into more trouble in the sense that we spent a lot of the daytime sat at home chilling out – just as we'd done when we were all still at secondary school. It was like an endless summer on constant repeat.

But the stakes were edging higher. Where my weed habit was relatively harmless apart from a few bad trips, my taste for cocaine wasn't. Cocaine made me feel alive and present at the beginning. I loved chasing the feeling of being permanently on edge. It made me feel powerful in the most visceral sense. I couldn't get enough of what people who use cocaine or speed call 'gurning' – where the jaw is working in a perpetual state of motion akin to chewing gum. And that position inevitably led to a situation whereby I was no longer just enjoying the stuff; I was now abusing it.

On the night of Saturday 31 July 2011, I was arguably at the peak of my drinking, drug-taking and fighting days.

From what I recall, that particular day – one of my friends' birthdays – was one of those super-hot, cloudless summer days where I felt happy to be alive, and excited to get properly 'on it' with a reason to celebrate.

I had a bit of money in my pocket and a few friends and myself were all planning to go out in Nottingham city centre. First, we assembled at somebody's house, snorted a few lines of coke and started drinking before we even went out. One of the older lads who was out with us was doing quite well for himself at the time and was a bit flash with the cash, as I recall – saying, 'I'll look after you for the day,' to people like me.

From there we headed to West Bridgford, a posh residential area nearby, and it was here that the older friend started buying everyone champagne, while we all went back and forth to the toilets to snort cocaine.

Although I had some money of my own from either my weed-selling exploits or whatever I'd managed to scrounge off my mum, I never had champagne kind of money, so I can't deny that it felt great to be an accepted part of this group. The sun was beating down, there were girls around, the city was packed and energetic because the cricket between England and India was on at the nearby Trent Bridge stadium. Everything about the day was set up to be a big one.

As the evening approached, after we'd spent the day hopping from pub to pub drinking and doing line after line, we all ended up back at the house of the friend whose birthday it was that day. There we continued drinking vodka now (cheaper), steadily losing touch with reality, while at the same time deciding what to do next.

Once we decided, we all set off. I swear to God there were probably 20 of us – all on various drugs. And just like any other night when we all went out, I'm sure more than one of us was saying, 'I can't wait to get in a fight tonight.'

A lot of the time we went to the same bars in Nottingham. Over the years we'd been to almost all of them, establishing not only where we'd even be allowed in (I witnessed a lot of racism directed towards my black and mixed-race friends by pub doormen), but also what kind of girls went there: students, well-to-do girls from posh areas of the city or normal girls from neighbourhoods like our own. We gravitated to wherever we thought our best chances lay.

We were at one of our usual haunts and from what I remember someone slipped a pill – half an ecstasy – in both my and the birthday boy's drinks. What a game-changer that was. There I was, eight hours into a session, having been drinking all day and taking cocaine. Now I had ecstasy in my system as well. Things got a bit hazy.

Looking back, the whole of that day is a bit blurry. I only remembered later that I was actually in a fight much earlier that day, on Trent Bridge itself. As this group of people walked by, one of them barged into my mate. My mate then got into a scrap and I jumped straight into the fray too. A tussle ensued on the bridge until eventually one of our group said, 'Come on, it's the middle of the day. The last thing we want is to get arrested before we've even been out for the night.'

We all looked at each other, agreed, and then we ran off like crazy people, on to the next bar. With drugs and alcohol in my system, I was already hyper and itching for some kind of confrontation – even by midday.

Anyway, as we reached town that night, as was often the case, the group started fragmenting because people went to meet various friends or chase girls to other bars or whatever. During the evening, we were all still in touch by phone, as we always were, saying where we were and how things were going, with the ultimate plan being to get back together by the end of the night.

By around 1 a.m., having got precisely nowhere with a girl I quite liked, I had lost almost all of my friends. Then my phone rang. One of my mates was on the line. I was told something was kicking off.

'We're at Market Square; where are you?'

'I'm just up the road on St James's Street.'

I put my drink down and ran out of the bar in the direction of Market Square.

This kind of call for help wasn't unusual when one or more of us was getting into a fight. But the thing that was different about this particular night was that, instead of being in the midst of a fight calling others for help, it was my mates who needed me – so I immediately went to get stuck in, albeit with false information.

I ran down the street, pulse quickening with every step, to Market Square. When I arrived, it was immediately apparent where things were kicking off; there was an obvious commotion outside a place called Yates's Wine Lodge. I heard shouting, drunken arguing; I didn't know what any of it was about.

I saw my mate butting foreheads with a lad. My mate had his fisted clenched and looked like he was going to punch him. But from out of nowhere, my mate's girl grabbed him from behind and pulled him away.

At that moment, I ran in from the side and punched the lad who'd been squaring off to my mate. I didn't plan it and I didn't think about it. I was acting on pure instinct – not to do physical damage, but simply to continue proving myself to my mates who had called for my help.

As the punch landed, it felt completely different to every other punch I'd ever thrown in my many years of drunk street-fighting. Usually when you punch someone, they stagger back or lean into you, or, of course, punch you back. From there the scuffle continues: someone else jumps in, you break your wrist on someone's head or so forth.

But none of these things happened that night.

I knew I had knocked this lad out instantly, and that was a feeling I'd never experienced previously, as often as we'd discussed the idea of a one-punch knockout from a macho standpoint within our group.

As soon as this punch landed, it was as if its impact instantly sobered me up. Having been in this crazed and dazed state in the aftermath of a day's worth of sun, drink, drugs and the ecstasy, suddenly the haze cleared as I thought, 'Shit. That was not supposed to happen.'

There I was, in the middle of Nottingham's Old Market Square, having just punched a lad who I'd instantly knocked unconscious, with an array of cameras everywhere. I didn't even look down at what had happened to the lad.

I now know he was called James Hodgkinson.

I didn't see him hit the floor. Instead, I turned and ran off, thinking, 'I'm not fucking hanging around here.'

There was no rationale whatsoever to my just fleeing the scene. I wasn't thinking of any consequences in that moment. All I knew was that I didn't want to get caught. I had no idea that the victim's father chased me. I only found out when he told me later that he would have tried to kill me if he had caught up with me.

For the next few minutes, God knows how many it was, I just kept running through the city in blind panic. As I got further away from the scene, I started veering off the main thoroughfares and down the various back alleys so as not to be picked up on camera or be caught by police. I hid in phone boxes and behind skips as I tried to navigate my way out of the city centre and back home to The Meadows as surreptitiously as I could.

At one point I stopped running altogether, sat down behind a restaurant's bin area and called my friends to find out where they were and what was happening. Really, I wanted to know if they were still at the scene of the punch. I remember speaking to this girl. It would have been at least 15 minutes after I left Market Square.

'He's still on the floor, Jacob,' she told me.

As I heard this news, I felt my heartbeat elevate with suffocating fear and panic.

Then, a minute or so later, a text came in from another mate that said, 'He's awake. He's being sick, now.' As I saw those words, I breathed the biggest imaginable sigh of relief. That he was okay was all I wanted to know. I thought that was the end of it.

As that knowledge permeated my addled mind, in my head that fight – if you can even call it a 'fight' – on 31 July 2011 just became like any other scuffle I'd been in at various times in the preceding three or four years. I made my way home thinking nothing more of it.

The next morning, when I saw my hung-over mates, they were all giving it, 'Ayyy, here's the one-punch man.'

Instead of being in any way affected by the previous night's incident, they were joking and congratulating me about what I'd done. At that point, other than my mates bragging about the punch, the night was no more remarkable than any other. I just thought everything would be fine.

My memory is a bit patchy, but I think that for the next couple of weeks, I carried on more or less as usual: going out at night, smoking weed during the day, playing PlayStation and, probably, getting into the odd fight or two on the weekend. Other than the day after the punch when my friends came round to big me up, we never discussed the events of 31 July again.

In the second week of August, my mum, my brother Sam and I went to Tenerife for a week. This was one of those occasions when my mum probably spent money she didn't really have. As it turned out, it was the last holiday we ever went on together as a family.

Fortunately, for all of us, it was perfect. While I was out there, I had the most idyllic time. We went swimming at water parks, went on a boat trip to see whales and dolphins, and ate nice food together. Other than a couple of nights when I met people from my neighbourhood who were also in Tenerife at the time, it was as if my relationship with mum briefly reverted back to how it had been before I went to secondary school and everything went bad.

For once, having been removed completely from the environment that had been informing my behaviour and, by extension, the fraught relationship I had with my mum, in Tenerife for those few days I felt comfortable with the idea of letting go of the persona I'd been developing for the preceding five years. My mum was completely different too. She was so much more relaxed.

When I got home from holiday the following Friday, everything still felt good. I was so much calmer and had renewed hope that maybe – after all – life could play out a lot more harmoniously than it had been up until then. Better still, it was the weekend. I had a nice, even suntan, and I went out on the Saturday night in Nottingham with my mates as usual.

Then the mood changed.

On the Sunday morning, one of the same guys who had come round to congratulate me on the punch, phoned me from work and told me that the police had just showed up at his house while he was on his way there.

At this point his brother, who had answered the door, had given him a heads-up. My friend, assuming that the police were already on their way to his workplace, was tipping me off that they'd probably be looking for me soon enough too.

Meanwhile, I was none the wiser about what was going down. More irritated than anything else by the inconvenience of having to answer the phone at all on a Sunday morning while feeling under the weather, I said to him, 'What the fuck are you telling me this for?'

'I think it might have something to do with when you punched that guy,' he said.

'What the fuck? I've got a hangover. Why are you putting this shit in my head?' is what I actually replied. But what I was really thinking was, 'Oh God, please don't let it be to do with that night ...'

The fear in my friend's voice got me paranoid. That phone call was the first time since 31 July that I'd even considered there might have been a tragic outcome to that night.

Then, when I got another call from a different friend's family to tell me that their son had been arrested, I went even further into panic mode, even though they didn't say what he'd been charged with specifically.

In fact, I can't be totally certain as to when I first found out that James had died as a result of the punch. It must have been around this time when the police were closing in, but I can't be completely sure.

Regardless of what I knew and when, the facts were that James was taken to hospital in Nottingham after regaining consciousness. The following morning, after a brain scan, he was taken for surgery.

He died in hospital nine days later.

In my mind, I started replaying every detail of 31 July over and over. And I'm ashamed to say that while I did, I was only looking at that night from my perspective. If something terrible had happened and the lad had died, I only needed two pieces of information. One, what material evidence was there to attach me to the incident? And two, what could I possibly do to conceal it?

Until they read a draft of this book I had never told James's parents that this is how I was feeling at the time, nor have I discussed it publicly until now. However, once I embarked on the journey of documenting all of these events and thoughts in a book, I knew that the only option available to me was to tell the absolute truth, no matter how unpalatable it is.

And the truth is that in the immediate aftermath of my learning about James Hodgkinson's death, my thoughts were not with him, or with his family, but only with how I could escape the blame for what happened. A young man had died because of my actions, but I wanted to get away with it. All my thoughts were selfish at this stage.

I started scrolling through pictures I'd been tagged in on Facebook and noting what clothes I'd been wearing on that night out. I immediately went home to my bedroom at my mum's house, located and disposed of all those items in question. Simultaneously, I asked people to un-tag me from everything on Facebook and started wholesale deleting of all my own posts from around that time.

As rash as all this might sound, I was in such a state of panic that these acts of amateur subterfuge were all I could think of to mitigate the situation. But at the same time, I knew there was a broader picture that was going to be much harder to conceal. All the time I was thinking, 'Yeah, but it was the bloody city centre. There are bound to be CCTV images of me everywhere.'

Again, I'm not proud of any of this, but I actually went to the city centre and retraced whatever steps I could remember taking from that night. As I walked, I looked at where the various cameras were and calculated the likelihood of my image being caught on any of them, given that I was pretty sure that it was CCTV images that had led the police back to my friends in the first place. Many of them had stayed at the scene and, ultimately, had their names taken by the police outside a nearby McDonald's an hour or so after the altercation.

These weren't irrational acts of mine – far from it. They were the highly calculated decisions of a desperate person whose sole aim was to evade the clutches of the law. However, when I stood in Market Square, yards from the scene of the punch, I recall feeling a sinking sense of futility.

Looking at the street corners where units sat atop traffic lights and where other cameras swivelled from mountings on the sides of buildings that overlooked the square, all I could think was, there are so many bloody cameras here. There are bound to be CCTV images of me.

While I was trying to establish what evidence was out there, unbeknownst to me, the investigation had clearly been moving forward.

This fact was confirmed when, later that day, I met up with my older mate who'd been out with us that night, and also the father of the friend of mine who'd been arrested by the police. It was at this point that the father told me his son had been arrested for James' murder.

I had to sit down. My mouth went dry.

My worst fears had been confirmed and my state of panic went into overdrive.

Although he'd been to prison himself, the father was understandably very distressed about all this. At the same time he told me that, according to what he'd been told by his son's solicitor, his boy was just giving the police 'no comment' responses to anything they asked him. 'I don't want my son being done for murder. You've got to tell me the truth. What happened?' he kept saying.

At this point, I started trying to reassure the man. 'You've got nothing to worry about,' I told him. 'He didn't do it.'

From there, the older friend and my mate's dad, both of whom had been in prison, found me down by the embankment steps on the River Trent, where I had learnt to fish and ride a bike. I still go and sit in the same spot from time to time. And they basically started giving me advice about what was likely to happen at every stage and what I should be doing to protect myself . At this point the reality truly sank in.

Their narrative slanted towards the idea that I hadn't meant to kill anyone and that therefore I shouldn't go down for murder.

'It'll probably be reduced down to manslaughter because you didn't intend to do it, but you need to come to terms with the fact that you'll still probably go to prison,' the dad told me.

Then he advised that the best thing I could do in the circumstances was to hand myself in and get myself the same solicitor as his son had.

As I walked, one of the drug-dealer 'burner' phones I still had in my possession rang. The number calling was the landline of my mum's house. I answered. It was the police on the other end.

Right then, I knew my time was up.

Even so, with the net closing, I took the sim cards out of both the phones I had and threw all the components in the river. I thought, 'Fuck, they're going to get me anyway ...'

Jacob Dunne

Now I had two choices, given that they'd raided my mum's house but had not yet released my two friends who they'd earlier arrested. I could go on the run, which would obviously have been irrational and would have merely delayed the inevitable. Or I could hand myself in, see what evidence the police actually had on me, and take my chances from there.

I briefly assessed what going on the run in Nottingham at the age of 19 would actually look like, and there was nothing whatsoever glamorous about it. I'd be sleeping on friends' sofas in a state of perpetual paranoia. I'd have no money and no resources of any kind. I thought about how long I could realistically live like that. A week? Maybe two? It felt pointless – and in any case, I'd only have been running from the truth.

So, instead of going home to my mum's house in The Meadows, I turned around and walked in completely the opposite direction.

Twenty minutes later I arrived in front of Bridewell Police Station, where some of my friend's family were gathered outside. They started crying and hugging me as I met them. They knew why I was there. I would walk in and their son would walk out shortly afterwards. I was handing myself in.

Chapter Four

Trial and Punishment

For all that my friend's dad had tried to reassure me and tell me what was likely to happen in the sense that I'd probably end up serving some time in jail, I don't think the gravity of my situation truly hit home to me until I sat in the interview room and was told by the detectives that I was being arrested for questioning about the murder of a 28-year-old young man called James Hodgkinson.

I suspected I was totally screwed and that there was no way out of what was coming to me. But, there was still a tiny part of me that hoped that I could still evade responsibility somehow – walk away and carry on with my life of zero accountability – especially if whatever evidence they had was insufficient to make a potential charge against me stick.

I thought through the possibilities carefully. Maybe there were no conclusive CCTV images of me after all? Maybe they were relying on a couple of unreliable witness statements? I had no idea what they really had, so a part of me was cautiously optimistic, even after I'd processed the seriousness of the charge I was potentially faced with.

At first I started by just giving them 'no comment' responses, knowing that my friend had done exactly the same. Because they could only technically hold me for 48 hours before they had to charge me or release me, my solicitor was asking questions like: 'What evidence do you actually have? Why are you still holding my client?'

'We're just waiting for CCTV images,' the police said, sounding confident that such images were on their way.

However, it turned out they didn't have CCTV images that were sufficient to charge me with anything. By some miracle, the cameras on the timers had moved at the right times and I wasn't picked up by any of them.

So, although I was the prime suspect, you could argue that the police had jumped the gun a little. The only option they had was to apply to a magistrate for an extra 12 hours on top of the 48, but rather than hold me for those 12 hours, they released me so that technically they could use the extra time the next day. By that time they hoped they might have new evidence.

I was sent home with instructions to return the following morning, on the various conditions that I surrendered my passport, wouldn't go on the internet – and a variety of other stipulations that I can't quite recall. I was sent home for the night and my solicitor dropped me off at my mum's house. It was a reprieve, but only a temporary one.

Three days previously, when the police raided my mum's house, they had gone through all the drawers in my bedroom looking for the clothes that were identified on the various witness statements from mates and the girls. Apparently they also took computers and any other electronic devices that were lying around in the house.

Initially my mum thought that the search was something to do with the London riots, which had spread to Nottingham city centre that August. The Meadows Police Station had been attacked. But I distinctly remember her saying, watching footage of the riots on television while we were in Tenerife on our idyllic holiday in the sun, 'I'm so glad you're not in the UK right now.'

Many of my mates had been involved in the trouble in Nottingham. Shops like JD Sports and Foot Locker were looted by marauding groups of youths and the stolen spoils ended up in bedrooms all over the city. She thought I might have been harbouring stolen goods and all I remember thinking was, 'Oh God, if only it was that …'

I was sitting there panicking, trying to find a way to tell my mum why the police had really called around when the local East Midlands news came on. The lead story was that a 19-year-old youth from The Meadows had been arrested on suspicion of murder. My mum looked at me and the penny dropped.

'Please don't tell me that's you they're talking about?' she said, with a look of abject horror on her face.

This was when I first had to break the news to her. I could no longer deny my role. Her reaction was absolute bloody pandemonium. She was angry, worried, upset and even slightly deluded – all at the same time. She actually thought I was lying to save my friends.

'You couldn't have done this, Jacob. I know that you're covering up for your mates,' she kept saying.

'No Mum, I'm not. Honestly,' I told her.

The next morning when I went back to the police station, they presented me with my other friend's statement – the guy whose brother had first phoned me to give me the heads-up about the police raid at his house.

Nobody, including me, had heard from him in the days prior to my handing myself in, and now I could see why, based on what was in the folder on the table in front of me. Clearly he'd been pulled in and had gone into huge detail in a statement to the police: people, times, places. He'd given them everything, including the names and addresses of the various girls who were with us that night. There was pages of the bloody stuff.

Also unknown to me, and this made matters worse, the police had also pulled in all of these girls and given them a proper good grilling. The girls added even more to the picture of that night by telling the police their detailed version of events: where we went, who was there and at what time.

The police had everything on me.

Although nobody had specifically named me in the statements as the perpetrator, my various friends and acquaintances had quietly sold me out to protect themselves by presenting a situation whereby it couldn't have been anyone else but me.

Now, there was no missing evidence or grey areas that might cast sufficient doubt on the situation for the police to not pursue a charge.

At the time I was absolutely raging about it all. I knew loads of people who'd got away with all kinds of crimes and just carried on with their lives. I'd been betrayed – which was an absolute no-no in our culture as far as I was concerned – and because of that it looked like my life was going to change for ever.

However, as unfair as I thought my situation was, I had no choice but to plead guilty when they eventually charged me.

'You should expect anything between three and eight years,' my solicitor told me.

There's a big difference between the two, I remember thinking.

Meanwhile, my solicitor went to court and pleaded my case – telling the judge that I wasn't a prolific offender and that I'd fully complied by handing in my passport and such like. Basically, he argued that I should be released back into the community, albeit with a security tag, until my court sentence date, which was more than two months away on 4 November 2011.

And that's what happened.

I was released, and for the next month or so I lived at my mum's house under strict curfew conditions.

At the same time my mum's frame of mind spiralled out of control. By that point she was already a fair way down the road with her alcoholism. But within a matter of days, the atmosphere in the house became absolutely awful. She was constantly accusing me of lying, and because she was so worried on my behalf, she wouldn't even let me bloody sleep. Nothing she said made any sense.

On reflection, knowing how compassionate a person my mum was, I'm sure she was extremely conflicted when she first heard this terrible news about her first-born son. On one hand, I'm sure she was desperately worried for me – her little boy. On the other, I don't doubt there was an equal part of her thinking,

'What about the other mum? How will she cope with losing her son like this?'

It was a mess of confused emotions. As much as I wanted everything to be harmonious before I went to prison, we just weren't equipped to have the kind of conversations that could make things any better. Drinking was obviously her way of making the worries disappear temporarily and it ultimately took her life.

Personally, I didn't have any headspace for worry at this point anyway. I was spending all of my time trying to deal with her. And now that I couldn't do what I'd always done – leave the house to escape her – I was losing patience.

Honestly, looking back, I'd much rather have gone to prison immediately and at least started serving my sentence, rather than staying in that house for a moment longer with my mum. I just wanted the process of punishment to begin.

In the end, as a compromise to make life easier, I arranged for my electronic tag to be relocated to my friend's house in a nearby part of The Meadows.

Although I didn't want to leave my brother Sam, who was actually more pissed off because all the electronic devices in the house had been removed than anything else (partly because having that connection to other worlds was a coping mechanism for him, he says), I just couldn't get out of there quickly enough for my own sanity's sake. There was nothing worse than watching my mum deteriorate like she was. I simply couldn't cope with it. I didn't go back.

As the court date approached, I wrote a letter to the judge asking whether, if deemed appropriate, it could be passed along to James Hodgkinson's family. I honestly can't remember the exact wording of this letter; I wrote it in the middle of the night in a rare moment of serenity.

All I know is that I tried to be as sincere as I possibly could. I did mean everything I said and I sent it with no expectation whatsoever of it making a difference to my sentence. I'm not even sure if the family ever got it. All I was thinking at the time of writing was, 'Maybe this is one thing I can actually do right?'

In court, I knew when I walked in that James's family were in the courtroom, and I recall feeling paranoid about that when I first entered the dock.

Once I was there, I couldn't even look at them. I was embarrassed and to look at them would only have made my situation real. Only a limited number of seats were available to family in the court and I remember looking around and seeing Mum, Sam, Nan and my aunty. Dad and my uncles Anthony and Brendan were also there.

Then I saw my friends and some of their family members. The rest of the court was made up of a bunch of random people, unconnected to the case, but who were clearly there to be nosey – to get some of the inside gossip on the local boy. I even saw someone from down the road sitting there and I remember thinking, 'What the fuck is she doing here? That should be one of my relatives.'

As the hearing progressed, increasingly aware that the eyes of all those in James's family were burning into me, I decided to just put my head down and stare at the floor. I detached from reality – pretty much the whole of the court proceedings – to the extent that, as I was getting taken down at the end of the hearing, I didn't even register that it had ended. I actually had to ask the prison officer who'd been sat next to me in the dock what sentence I'd received.

That's how out of it I was that day – and I genuinely think that's what people do when they're in a situation they can't process. They just retreat into their own head and start locking the world out – as I found myself doing throughout most of my days at secondary school, as the ADHD (and other) labels stuck.

With hindsight, being mentally absent was a coping mechanism that I'd unwittingly been relying on my whole life. Sometimes it served me well, like when my mum was kicking off drunk and in my ear. But more often it put me in a state of inertia. Coping by not coping meant that I never developed any means of dealing with my thoughts and emotions. I was numb. And then, because it was weak to even acknowledge that you had thoughts or feelings in the culture I grew into, what chance did I have of processing difficult emotions or triggers when sat in a crowded courtroom awaiting a prison sentence?

Anyway, I was sentenced to slightly more than 30 months. Some time was taken off because I'd been on the tag for those two months in the community. It wasn't until I was downstairs waiting to go to prison that I found out the sentence. I didn't even take in what was being said in the court room and relied instead on the officer who escorted me from the room. But when I first heard this news, my first thought was, 'Well, that's actually quite good.'

I soon realised that, as lenient as it might have seemed relative to what it could have been (my sentence was at the lower end according to the guidelines), I still had to go to prison, and, while I'd acquired some anecdotal background knowledge from various friends over the years, I had no real concept of what having my liberty taken away was going to be like for me.

I was about to find out.

HM Prison Nottingham is in the Sherwood area of the city, which is only a 10-minute drive through town from the Crown Court.

In addition to being a holding prison, HMP Nottingham is also a remand prison for people who are awaiting future court appearance dates. Some inmates were first-timers like me; others were habitual criminals who were being churned around by the system.

Right from the start, I knew my stay in HMP Nottingham would be temporary. It was always understood that, after an initial stay of a few weeks, I would be moved to a young offender institution to serve out the rest of my sentence. I was well aware that these two types of facilities would be completely different in nature, for reasons I'll explain.

Regardless, when I arrived I had to go through the standard HM Prisons' induction process: fingerprints, mug-shot – as well as a naked search while sitting on a plastic chair to make sure that I hadn't smuggled drugs or a phone up my arse.

Initially I was taken to an induction wing, where my cell was located on the ground floor of 'C' Block. The layout looked much like old-school Victorian-style prisons you see on television shows: three storeys high with metal staircases on either side of a main hall that led to long corridors on each level protected with nets in the middle to stop people from jumping off.

I was led into my room and as the door slammed behind me like it does in crime dramas on television I remember initially being shell-shocked by the reality that I was now incarcerated.

This particular cell was a single (many were double, which two inmates shared) and so there was only a single bed position against the wall on one side. In total, it was probably only nine feet in length from the door to the window at the other end, which looked out onto the prison yard.

There was a toilet, a little table and a cupboard for any belongings, which by that time didn't amount to much. All I had to my name was the 'welcome' bag I was given upon induction, which comprised a few essential bits and pieces: tobacco (not really 'essential' and readily available in prison anyway), toothbrush, plastic knife and fork, and a multi-purpose food bowl.

Meanwhile, any other belongings I had with me in court had been removed and stored until my release date. In place of any clothes I'd worn to court, I was given the standard-issue maroon tracksuit synonymous with the induction wing.

I was surprised to discover that there was a TV in my room. On that first early evening, while I lay down on the bed just trying to stay calm about my situation, I flicked the television on and saw Will Smith in *The Fresh Prince of Bel-Air*.

Despite my circumstances, I actually found myself laughing out loud a few times as I watched. I was just a few hours into a 14-month sentence, so it was a bit surreal to find myself laughing in my cell. I remember thinking, 'If people knew this they'd probably assume I'm a lunatic ...'

Shortly after the programme finished, I started seeing and hearing fireworks outside the window of my prison cell. Just over the wall from the prison was a housing estate and people were obviously letting off fireworks for bonfire night from their gardens, but because of the depth of my self-pity at that time, in my mind I twisted these simple family firework displays into believing that they were actually society's way of celebrating that I was in prison and no longer their problem.

Next I remember being released from my cell for food for the first time, at around 6.30 p.m. that evening. They let out one floor of the prison wing at a time, and then I walked along the corridor and queued in a line at a canteen not unlike what you might find in department store cafes, minus the luxury touches such as nice furniture and carpets.

As I was deciding what I wanted to eat before taking my tray back to my cell, one of the people serving the food did a double-take at me. I could see the moment of recognition in his eyes.

'You're that guy who punched the lad, aren't you? I just saw you on the news,' he said, pointing at me at the same time.

'Yeah,' I said, without knowing what this person's take on it all would be.

And then I realised that, because East Midlands news must have just been on, the word was probably already out in the prison about who I was and what I'd done. It was in those moments – as I walked back to my cell with chicken that still had feathers on it – that I really started to process what the next year or so was going to look like. People were going to know me. Many would be aware of the details of the crime I committed. Information spreads like wildfire. That's just how prisons are. There's not much else to do but gossip about other people's business.

I was on this induction wing for only two days. It was quiet; nobody was settled because they knew they'd be moving somewhere else. There was no established culture.

Then I was moved to another part of the prison and, as if moving wasn't hard enough, I had to walk onto a wing where every person was wearing a grey tracksuit, dressed in clothes – the maroon outfit – that made it blatantly obvious to everyone that I was new. As soon as I arrived, I stuck out like a sore thumb.

Now I had to decide how I was going to approach this new environment. Before I went to prison and was in the community on the tag, people were giving me all kinds of advice, whether I liked it or not. 'Don't let nobody take you for a dickhead in there, Jacob', or, 'Make sure you let people know that you'll put up a fight.'

Confronted with such advice, I remember thinking, 'Oh man, I hope it doesn't come to that …'

I suppose that I was already quite good at this 'running with the hounds and hunting with the hares' approach, given. I'd become good at building rapport and adapting to different circumstances and social groups. If I had to do it again, I knew that I could.

But I knew that doing so was going to be exhausting. Honestly, I really didn't want to expend the energy of having to put up some façade or other, every day. I'd been living a chameleon life for years: seeking affirmation from some, ingratiating myself with others. I did it because I had to. However, now that I was actually in prison and not on the street, part of me had hoped that I could just let the days and weeks pass with no drama.

At the beginning, I genuinely think I believed I could stay out of any prison culture altogether for the entire duration of my sentence. 'Surely I can just do my own thing?' I thought.

But I soon realised that that was a completely unrealistic expectation. It's impossible not to project some kind of aura.

So, having assessed the situation over a couple of days, seen a few people out and about on the wing, tried to establish if there was anyone from my neighbourhood and got a rough feel of what I was up against, I decided that I would take a measured and moderate approach to things instead of just being inert.

I wasn't going to go around staring people out and trying to prove how hard I was. I knew that would only lead to confrontation and I understood enough about prison culture to recognise that getting into trouble would then lead to a removal of privileges. Not just that, I also knew that many of the people in adult prisons were total units.

Equally, it made no sense to keep my head down 24/7 in an attempt to be invisible. In an environment like prison, that would make me look weak. And again, based on what I'd been told in the weeks prior to my incarceration, I understood that, in prison, the weak just don't survive. Specifically in youth offending prisons – adult prisons are relatively calmer in comparison.

After two or three weeks in HMP Nottingham, I actually started thinking, 'This is okay!'

For some reason, because there was every Tom, Dick and Harry in there from every age range, the place didn't seem too hostile. For all that I was mentally resisting being there, I slipped into the routine of prison life while still in a state of shock.

On my exercise breaks, where we were just allowed to walk around a fenced-off area for an hour a day, I literally didn't know what to do with myself to start with. It felt like the first day at school again. I knew nobody; I had no mobile phone screen to stare at when I walked past somebody who I didn't want to talk to. In prison, you are forced to engage with yourself or to socialise with other people in a way that you just aren't in modern normal society. It really made me realise how much we rely on mobile phones as a way to disengage, as much as we use them to engage socially.

As it turned out, there were a couple of lads from my area on that wing – but I didn't know either well and they were both a little older. Not having anyone else I wanted to talk to on these exercise breaks, we talked for that hour, cross-referenced people we knew in common, but that was it. We returned to life in our own cells for the other 23 hours.

Fortunately, for half of the time I was on the new wing, I was in a cell on my own. But I was moved to a cell that had two bunk-beds instead of the single bed I'd had on the induction wing, and this meant one thing: a new cellmate. Although I'd only experienced a few days of prison life, I knew this would be a different dynamic.

My main fears were that (a) I'd have to share a cell with an absolute nutter and (b) that I'd somehow get put with someone from a rival area of Nottingham who didn't get along with guys like me.

Neither of those scenarios appealed. I knew I could survive on my own if I could control my own immediate environment. But with someone else like that in a nine-foot-long cell, things would naturally become much harder to manage. And they did.

After a couple of weeks, this scruffy-looking lad from Mansfield was brought in. At first glance, I wasn't sure about him at all. Let's face it – I would have been suspicious of anybody at that point. I'd been operating in a culture where nobody outside of my immediate circle of friends was to be trusted. But while he looked like a tramp and was a bit scabby, it could have been a lot worse. Fortunately, after an initially awkward settling-in period together, where we both feel self-conscious about going for a shit or whatever else in the other's company, this lad from Mansfield turned out to be alright. It quickly became obvious that, despite his unkempt appearance, he wasn't the type to come in and cause any trouble.

Inevitably we got into all kinds of conversations about life and how we ended up sharing a cell together. It's surprising how quickly, just because of a shared predicament that neither of us could control, we slipped into a weirdly comfortable routine: timing exercise hours so that the other could shit in peace, watching the same TV programmes each day at the same time. Looking back, I really valued this guy's company, short though our time together was in the scheme of things.

When I wasn't sitting there talking to this lad about life and the intricacies of the *EastEnders* plot, I was using the little notebook I'd taken in with me containing all my friends' and family's phone numbers and addresses. I had no money, so I couldn't make any phone calls. Instead, I managed to get hold of a couple of stamps to send letters.

But the relative comfort of HMP Nottingham soon came an end and I was moved to a young offender institution in Leicestershire called HMP Glen Parva.

People might assume that this would be a more relaxed environment than a full-blown prison like HMP Nottingham. That wasn't not the case.

There was an airy, transient feel to Nottingham. People were there on remand; there was a broad range of inmates from across the age spectrum, many of whom were already quite well versed in the nuances of prison life and were perfectly accepting of it all. Honestly, as prisons go, it was relatively calm.

But I knew a young offender institution would be totally different scenario. Like me, many of these lads would be experiencing their first taste of incarceration and would be pushing back hard against it. Because everyone was young, testosterone-fuelled and disillusioned by life in regular society to the extent that they'd run out of outlets by which to express their dissatisfaction, it stood to reason that many of them would likely be kicking off and starting fights every day just to prove something.

As I sat in the minibus on the way to this new facility with the two or three others who were being transported the same day, I can't deny that I was extremely unsettled about what lay ahead at the end of the hour-long drive in this 'sweat box' south to Leicester across the Trent Bridge. For a moment I caught a glimpse of my family home as we passed Bathley Street and my heart sank. I knew this was where my sentence would truly begin.

I arrived at Glen Parva a month after I'd been booked into Nottingham, and I had to go through an induction process all over again: strip-searched, photographed, fingerprints, and issued with a prison number.

In prison, your prison number is your identity. It is you. In some places you might occasionally get away with giving your surname, but in general you are a number, and that series of digits and letters becomes ingrained in your psyche because it is your passport to everything. If you want to be let off the wing for whatever reason, you need your number. Going to education or the gym? Number.

In no way is it a cliché to say that a prison number has a dehumanising effect. In no time at all I started thinking of myself not as Jacob Dunne but only as my prison number. Thankfully I have forgotten it now – ironic considering how significant it was at the time.

As if to reinforce my worst fears I got put straight into a cell with a right bloody nutter. This lad must have been 18 and he spent the first night talking more shit in my ear than I'd ever heard in my life.

He reckoned he'd held up a post office with a gun somewhere and then been involved in some mad car chase with the police around the Midlands. He was one of those people – and there are a lot of them in prison – who just wanted to impress other people with how crazy his story was. And because you're in prison, with no access to the outside world, such stories are hard to verify.

To this day, I still don't know if what he told me was real. I think maybe his way of dealing with the social discomfort of being in a cell with me 24/7 was to talk exaggerated shit about what he'd done and how violent he could be.

I would never have admitted it at the time, but I was genuinely scared about this young offender institution at first. For all the reasons I've mentioned, it was such a different, far more intimidating environment.

Unlike the Victorian styling of the other prison, Glen Parva was newer and with a series of long, claustrophobic corridors, not unlike a hotel, with cells all the way along each. There were two or three levels of these corridors and it all seemed so much more intense and crammed-in than I'd experienced at HMP Nottingham.

When I walked down my corridor to the canteen on that first night, all these young gangsters were eyeing me up through the viewing holes of the cell doors as I walked past. 'Fresh meat,' I heard a few of them saying. Little did I know that, a few months later, I'd be doing exactly the same, as the negative culture of prison gradually rubbed off on me.

Meanwhile, it seemed as though everyone else was shouting crazy abuse out the doors of their cells. This insults seemed to be indiscriminate – directed at the universe in general as opposed to any person in particular. Even people who were having relatively 'normal' conversations seemed to be doing so in an aggressive and violent tone. I suppose that was all they knew.

When I got to the canteen, because I didn't know anybody at all, I sat down in one of the empty chairs that lined the room, trying to avoid the attentions of 'the chatty guy' who always seems to be there in schools and prisons on the first day. He was already straight in my ear. 'Alright mate? When did you get here?' he said, with unnervingly wild eyes.

'The last thing I want is this guy sticking to me from day one,' I thought.

It would be an inauspicious introduction to my new home's catering skills too. Because we'd arrived late and induction had taken more time than usual, all the food was either cold or gone altogether.

'We'll try to find you something,' the guy who was cleaning up the hotplates said with not much enthusiasm.

A few minutes later he came back with a jacket potato that had been reheated several times. With it were a few of the left-over, crunchy chips that nobody had wanted and some soggy coleslaw. As I sat there I remember sighing, feeling sorry for myself and thinking, 'For fuck's sake. Is this really what I've got to come?'

Later that first night I was allowed a phone call with my nan and all I can remember is that I could hear in her voice that she was trying so hard to be brave for me. Meanwhile, I was trying to do the same for her, but in the end I ended up just crying down the phone in despair thinking, 'How am I ever going to be able to do this?'

It's not on to show any weakness in prison, but I couldn't help myself as I sat in my cell bawling my eyes out (I could never have cracked in public) – simply because I didn't know how else to express my total despair about what my life had become. That evening was definitely one of my low points. It's when I knew I'd hit rock bottom.

In early December 2011, it would be fair to say that I could see no hope in my situation. All I kept thinking was, 'This time next year I'll still be here.'

Meanwhile, the nutter I was sharing a cell with had a bloody calendar up on the wall and was crossing days off it at the same time every day religiously.

'What's wrong with you?' I said after a while. 'I don't want to stare at that shit every day.'

'I can see the days going by,' he said.

'Yeah, but I want to forget about the bloody days,' I told him.

It didn't help that HMP Glen Parva had the general reputation for being the most violent young offender institution outside of London.

As if that wasn't bad enough, just as I got transferred there, a whole load of people who had been involved with the riots in some way or another were arrested and detained.

Because many of the London institutions were full, there was spillover to Glen Parva – which could house 800 offenders at any one time – and the demographic was all over the place.

In addition to people from the East Midlands, there were others from elsewhere in the Midlands, London and even from places like Doncaster and Sheffield. There were members from gangs from all over the country, but what that meant was that, because of the sheer mix of inmates, no one group for any area outnumbered any other.

Admittedly, some of these lads weren't exactly hardened criminals. In the aftermath of the riots, the police had simply widened the net and started pulling in all sorts of individuals, many of whom had probably never committed much of a crime in their life. I would eventually meet college students who had simply jumped on the riot bandwagon, smashed a couple of shop windows or nicked a pair of trainers, and got caught.

I met another guy who got four years for simply posting on Facebook that he was going down to House of Fraser when it was being looted. Because of a single post – far less an action – he got accused of being a social media ringleader/coordinator and received what seemed like a disproportionate punishment as a result. He was no criminal. He was as decent a lad as I'd ever met.

Inevitably, there were a couple of guys from the Nottingham area that I vaguely knew. One of them had got four years for stabbing someone in a fight. The other was in on a firearms charge of some kind. Although these two weren't from The Meadows specifically, I was immediately more drawn to them by virtue of the fact that they were at least from the same city as I was.

So, all of these people were part of this increased intake at the prison, and what I found was that institutions like Glen Parva have a way of reducing everybody – no matter what they thought they were on the outside – to the same level. And that level was one of low obedience.

Unless you were enrolled in some kind of education course or had a job, you were in your cell pretty much 23 hours of every day, isolated from everything and everyone, other than with two or potentially three other cellmates. That status is called 'basic' – and this level of prison rights/ living conditions applies to pretty much everyone in the UK prison population at any given time.

Most people in HMP Glen Parva didn't particularly want basic rights, however. Naturally, almost everyone wanted to be out and about on the wing at various levels of privilege, talking to people, playing table tennis, getting a shower, ordering stuff from the canteen once a week (shower gel, toothpaste, snacks and so forth), getting regular visits, being given more time for phone calls or just doing something to give each day some kind of purpose.

To be able to do these things, you had to qualify for what was called 'standard' privileges, and you became eligible for those if you behaved well and showed yourself willing to be respectful to prisoner officers and to work.

Some prisoners were allowed out of their cell for most of the day, to make as many phone calls as their finances allowed, and to play pool and such like. That level is called 'enhanced'. However, at one point while I was there the pool tables got taken away because one of the inmates kicked off about something and smashed a prison officer over the head with a pool cue.

One of the other desirable perks on 'enhanced' was that you were allowed to have your own clothes sent in from the outside. I personally never had any clothes sent in for the entire duration of my sentence because, although I always had a job, I never made it to enhanced status – simply because I didn't want to suck up to the prison officers sufficiently to get the points that would have moved me into a new and elevated bracket.

The reality was that, for me, there were so many things to get pissed off about when it came to the prison officers; I just never felt comfortable with kissing arse. Not just that, my attitude also meant that the officers had less power to take things away from me – something that they clearly enjoyed doing.

Furthermore, although I was in a correctional facility to change my thinking, there was a huge part of me that was still in that anti-authority mentality where it was the default position to rail against the system – a system that was characterised by anyone in uniform wielding positions of power. While I was among peers in prison – people I only barely knew but nevertheless shared a lot with – it stands to reason that I was always going to perpetuate the complete disrespect for authority that I'd shown since secondary school.

Instead of being corrected in any way, as time passed and my confidence increased, I got up to increasing amounts of no good by selling tobacco I bought with my nan's postal orders, and selling it to people for more than it was worth.

I inevitably got caught a few times and so I remained in basic, where I wore the standard-issue tracksuit every day along with the shoes I wore in court – a black pair of Fred Perry going-out shoes, which, by five months into the sentence, had several holes in both soles so that when I went outside, my feet got bloody wet. I went into prison in those shoes, and I'd leave in them 14 months later.

Truthfully, I never gave shoes, clothing or anything else that I might have cared about on the outside any thought in prison. I just got up every morning, put whatever I had on and started the day. For much of the time I was on autopilot, being carried along by a new set of rules.

As far as I could see, everyone was just trying to get into some kind of rhythm – a rhythm that would make their incarcerated life as normal and bearable possible. Most people genuinely just want to forget how long they've got and detach from everything that's going on in the outside world.

It took me around four months to accept my situation and to just commit to making the best of prison life. On reflection, it was a combination of factors that prevented me from settling in as quickly as others did.

First, although it's not common for people to discuss such things in male-orientated prison environments, I suspect that it's perfectly normal to wake up in the morning every day hating the situation you're in, and to perhaps feel bitter and resentful about why you are in it.

Given my specific circumstances – where I still felt that my friends had completely betrayed me – this was definitely true. I woke up feeling very down every day for a while, although the power of that emotion gradually weakened over time and everything became less distressing.

Second, for the first few months I was getting bombarded with so many letters from friends and family that it was impossible to detach from events on the outside even if I wanted to. In fact, the guidance for prisons is to encourage people to maintain contact with positive connections on the outside.

Personally, I felt that this was actually a little counterproductive in the sense that, by engaging in that stuff as a prisoner, all you find yourself doing is either thinking about what you're missing, stewing about what hurt and disappointment you've caused your loved ones, or simply telling people how shit life is on the inside. I did all of those things, sometimes all at once.

Also, if you go back and forth with someone often enough by mail or on the phone, sooner or later they'll begin to tell you about their life and problems, and at that point you start feeling bad about sharing with them anything negative about your life. None of this helps. It's a downward spiral that only breaks when the communication dries up. Then you start socially isolating yourself because it's less stressful to not deal with the outside at all.

My position wasn't helped by the fact that, in the background, there were other problems in my immediate family. As I mentioned, my mum was already struggling even before I went into prison. Now that I was actually there, her mental state had seemingly got much worse – according to my nan, who was telling me all of what was going on whenever I called her.

My mum was an Ofsted-registered childminder. She loved her job, was paid ok and was very good at it. But when the police came to arrest me back in 2011, all of that ended. She was told she could no longer continue working on account because she'd had a violent person living in her house.

Without her job, my mum soon got behind with her mortgage payments. Before long, she was forced to sell the house we'd grown up in and go into private renting. Life was falling apart, and drinking was her way of blocking it all out.

From what I could gather, she was in a right state with the drink from day to day. 'Your mum has been found outside on the street, drunk off her face,' Nan told me in one call. 'She had to be escorted home the other night by strangers,' she said in another.

Hearing all of this, I just felt helpless and angry because I was certain that everything was my fault – and at this point I was angry enough with my friends as it was. But from prison, there was literally nothing I could do to fix the situation. All I could do, other than be perpetually furious about the fact that I couldn't make her problems magically go away, was to offset that rage by writing calm letters to my mum now and again saying something along the lines of, 'Please don't worry about me, Mum. I will be fine. Please focus on looking after yourself and my little brother.'

That, unfortunately, was easier said than done for her, given how every part of her life had fallen apart. I was so concerned about her and Sam. If it was hard for me, I think it was tougher for him. He was younger, less worldly, and now he was forced to fend for himself as Mum went from being a functioning alcoholic, as so many are, to being a full-blown one in a matter of months. He had no choice but to grow up. Half the time he didn't even know where she was, as he spent a lot of time with my aunty and nan around this time.

For me, our family's financial status meant that I had fuck-all money to spend on luxuries for the entire time I was in prison. Other than the occasional twenty-pound postal order that Nan would send me from time to time, I had no money whatsoever. I can't even tell you how grateful I was to her for sending me those postal orders. They salvaged my sanity more than once.

Chapter Five

Glen Parva

I'm just trying to earn them diamonds – could call that
    shit blood diamond
not got a car but I'll be riding
on tag but I ain't hiding
got these olders acting weary and the youngers
    looking scary
taking all that fucking cream – call me Mr dairy
not much in life to live for so that money is what I bleed
    for – straight to the point no detour – Money straight
    no seesaw
I do it right but I don't need Nike but I love the message
    just do it
Mr Ronald says he loves it – I know he's talking
    'bout money.
so pull over it's my time, realest chick on my line, and I go
    in at the right time go in at that right time – champagne
    on the roadside

fuck a snitch that's my crime got a judge waving
bye-bye
2 to 3 that's my time but when I'm back it's game time.
                    Jacob Dunne – January 2012, HMP Glen Parva

I don't remember the precise transition point, but after a few months in prison there comes a time when you realise that all the conversations you are having are not about the life you used to have outside, but only about what's going on inside the walls of the prison and whatever you have access to that's worth discussing: what's on TV tonight, what was on TV last night and which female prison officers are the most attractive.

These TV-related chats were, of course, tedious. We literally watched every episode of every soap opera – to the extent that I'm sure that the ratings for these soaps owe a lot to prisons over the years, given that many of the c. 80,000 people in prison in the UK at any one time probably watch every episode. But at least the conversations changed every day because of the constantly evolving plots of these programmes. The longer you're in prison, the lower your standards drop.

My wider point is that you find yourself being drawn into micro-worlds that are mostly concerned with a limited list of subjects – the first being what's happening on each wing and what drama has ensued from it. Because all the prisoner officers carried radios with them, anytime you heard a siren going off on their radio loudspeakers, you knew that there was an incident somewhere on another wing of the prison and that officers were being summoned to attend as backup.

They would go running off the wing, and when they came back, we'd start asking questions like: 'Which wing did you go to?' or 'What happened there?'

We'd get all the gossip off these prison officers and then, when you went to the gym or to do work or whatever, you'd invariably speak to people from that wing and ask them all about it too.

Even though everyone was technically isolated in their own little room and sometimes only let out for an hour each day, any gossip or rumour spread like wildfire. That's just how prisons are. In the same way as people still manage to get drugs, tobacco and mobile phones inside despite all the security, the dissemination of information about what's going on anywhere in the prison in real time just can't be stopped either. The riots were talked about a lot, as well as *Crimewatch* and any notorious criminal fuck-ups that took place.

In addition to gossip about what's happening inside the prison, the main kinds of conversations that took place between prisoners were about how long each of us had left on our sentence and where we came from. On reflection, I think these conversations were really important – if for no other reason that some people genuinely took solace and got encouragement from the fact that others had longer than them to serve. If you had a year left and you talked to some lad who still had three and a half, then obviously you were going to feel better about it: knowing there's someone worse off doesn't make your sentence disappear, but it certainly makes it seem more manageable. Equally, if someone told you that they'd already managed to endure a sentence that was much longer than the one you were going to serve, you took comfort from that too. In prison, everything is relative.

Conversations about the specific nature of the crimes we each had committed came up at various times, also. In my case, whenever anyone asked me about my crime, I'd spend a short time talking about what I actually did – followed by a disproportionately long time explaining how I got caught and my associated grievances about how my friends screwed me over.

Nobody I ever discussed this with said, 'Maybe you're looking at this selfishly.' That's just not criminal mentality and people were always wary of digging too deep, especially in a case where there was a death involved.

Instead of playing devil's advocate, everyone just reinforced the negative feelings I had about my friends and the system, typically by saying stuff like, 'I can't believe your friend did that. I'd be bloody shooting him when I got out, if I were you.'

In all honesty, this feedback perfectly fitted my worldview at the time. At that moment, all I wanted to hear was that my negative feelings were justified and that I should be seeking revenge upon my release.

This attitude merely confirmed that I was miles away from any sense of objectivity about what I'd done. I felt as if I were the victim – that it was I who was enduring hard times and not James's family. Whenever anyone did ask me (and this was very rare), 'Do you ever think about the person who died because of you?', I'd instinctively say, 'No.'

This, however, was not true. Thoughts did occasionally enter my head – the picture of James that appeared in the local paper and on TV news, for example, frequently entered my mind's eye. But as quickly as these thoughts and images came to me, I would mentally recoil. Rather than dwell on them for too long and allow myself to form any association with them, I'd just push them away and distract myself with something else, simply to avoid dealing with the unpleasant reality.

When I couldn't distract myself, I'd get angry instead and say to myself, 'Fuck that. I'm not going there. I'm not opening that box.' I just wasn't equipped to process my guilt and shame in any other way.

Bizarrely, one of the prisoner officers even tried to engage with me about my crime at one point in my sentence. I'm not sure what his angle was, but what he did was walk into my cell holding a pile of news articles he'd printed off the internet, including all of the readers' comments.

'This is what the public thinks of you. What do you think of that?' he said, pointing at one of the pages of comments, some of which were damning to say the least.

Let's say that I did not respond positively to being put on the spot in this way. I was well and truly wound up.

'Who the fuck do you think you are, talking to me like this?' I said. 'I don't give a fuck about what anyone thinks.'

Obviously I did care, or else I wouldn't have been triggered (emotionally riled) by what he said and responded so defensively. But at the time I just wasn't equipped to discuss it in that way – a way that I thought was simply disrespectful.

Albeit that I might well have written similar comments myself under different circumstances, being shown the opinions of ill-informed people on the Internet was never going to get me to reflect on my crime in a constructive way. The way I saw it, I'd already been sent to prison and been forcibly disconnected from society. The system had already told me in no uncertain terms that I wasn't good enough to be in the normal world.

Now this guy was simply rubbing my nose in it further by confirming, in black and white, that in the opinion of anonymous strangers I was worthless and deserved no reprieve. If he was looking for some kind of contrition, he went about it the wrong way. I just wasn't having it.

All the prison officer's antics did was make me angrier and pushed me further away from ever wanting to be a part of normal society again. Instead of taking on any blame myself, I just felt further threatened and alienated by everyone else: my friends, my community, my family – and now the criminal justice system. In those moments looking at the comments, I felt like I had nobody.

Regardless of my bleak attitude, I somehow knew that it wouldn't help me to just sit around stewing in anger and self-pity: I would have completely self-destructed. So to distract myself, I knuckled down with prison work, and the job I liked best was working in the catering area – specifically on the servery counter, where you could stay away from your cell the longest and get better food for yourself.

Given there were so many inmates to feed, there was always work to be done. Not just that, there was a choice of shifts, either full-time, or just a morning part-time. I chose the latter, so sometimes, if my privileges permitted, I could either go to the gym in the afternoon or have my hour-long association break. People who worked full-time had their association break in the evening. This was a time when you could take a shower, make a call, play some table tennis or get some fresh air in the exercise yard.

'Movement' was when things often kicked off. Everyone obviously had to be locked up overnight, but in the morning we were all allowed out at 8.25 a.m. to get our breakfast, with just half an hour allocated to eat it in our cells. Thereafter, everyone who was going to work moved to wherever they were going, just before 9 a.m. – and that's when fights happened and illicit goods were exchanged between prisoners.

Drugs and mobile phones, despite being strictly prohibited, were plentiful in prison, and at the beginning I never fully understood how so many people got away with sneaking items inside.

However, with time I realised that, because the cells were so close together, people had worked out clever ways of passing stuff back and forth across the corridor or by using a 'line' of toilet paper attached to contraband, to be dangled out of the window and blown by the wind to the next cell's window. There were also many dodgy prisoner officers who were more than willing to make money on the side by exploiting inmate anguish.

It's part of the depressing reality of the UK prison system that these people could make 750 quid by bringing in a £10 phone for someone, who would then arrange for their family to pay the prisoner officer.

The truth is that people are so desperate for contact that they're willing to pay disproportionately large sums of money to keep lines of communication with the outside open. Knowing this, an unscrupulous prison officer could do a couple of phone transactions and have the equivalent of a month's wages on the side.

Equally, drugs routinely made their way into prison – smuggled by inmates themselves or by family members and friends showing up on visits.

Drugs were everywhere – arguably more prevalent than on the street. It was a joke, really. Although there was that strip-search on induction mentioned earlier, people still thought nothing of putting an ounce of weed up their arse, simply because they knew how much that would be worth to them on the inside.

The reality of the matter was that this ounce could set someone up financially in prison; they wouldn't be starting from rock bottom. A single joint could be exchanged for a packet of tobacco, and so on. I know that people shoved phones up their arses too, hoping not to get caught. The benefits vastly outweighed the risks.

It was only after I left prison that legal highs started becoming rife in prisons – particularly 'spice', as it's now called. Relative to weed and such like, these legal highs were so much easier to get through the various levels of security. They were tiny and odourless, so sniffer dogs didn't pick up a scent. They could even be melted onto paper and sent in on letters. For a while, prisoner staff had no clue what was going on.

This move to legal highs, I'm told, changed everything – and it's still happening now on a massive scale, simply because people are even more desperate for substances to ease their pain in prison than they are on the outside.

The sad truth is that addicts (and many prison inmates are addicts) are in pain, mentally, and prison conditions only enhance that pain. People therefore find any way they can to cope with that pain, even if that means putting their immediate health at risk. As a result, they will literally do anything – even if that means brewing dodgy alcohol concoctions in their cell or trying new types of drugs, the effects of which might be completely unknown.

Jacob Dunne

My coping mechanism did not include drugs or alcohol, however. On reflection, I think I used my festering anger more than anything else to get me through prison, as well as the ability I'd developed as a child to completely disassociate from everything around me. Having clear structured days and routines in prison probably helped ease a lot of my anxiety too.

As I said, I didn't go around looking for fights – that would have worked to my disadvantage in the sense that I would have had privileges limited and had much more drama to deal with, which in turn would have pissed me off further. But I definitely did make it very clear at every opportunity that I wasn't a push-over. Just like I did in the outside world on the street, I found what I thought was the right balance. Treating people how you want to be treated works just as well in prisons as anywhere else.

At various times during my sentence – while I was on the phone to family or in the canteen queue for food, for example – people took the piss out of me and then waited to see what my reaction was. If I gave the banter straight back, that sent a message: that I was confident in myself and would be no easy target. If I hadn't responded and had kept my head down, that would have sent another message altogether, and one that warranted further probing: that I was weak and worthy of exploitation.

It might sound petty in the scheme of things, but it really is the manner in which you approach these subtle exchanges that dictates how people relate to you in prison. And with hindsight, my experiences in gang culture definitely helped me navigate such interactions in the right way. I just had to ride the wave.

There comes a time in prison when you start thinking about what life is going to look like when you get out. For me, from memory, these thoughts started drifting into my mind, mainly in the still of night, once I'd been in prison for almost a year.

Just prior to that, there was a significant moment that is worth mentioning. While I didn't register it fully at the time, it did have some significance – albeit possibly only on a subconscious level.

On 31 July 2012, a year after the punch, the prison vicar came to me and asked if I'd like to accompany him to the chapel. I went, willingly and unthinkingly, and there I sat in silence and said a solemn and heartfelt prayer for James Hodgkinson.

Although my mum had a church background, I couldn't ever say that religion had been an important part of my life. I do think there has always been some faith hiding away in there somewhere, even if I only reverted to it in moments of absolute crisis, when I'd find myself inwardly saying something along the lines of, 'Fuck sake, God. Please, come on – help me!'

I can't tell you how good it felt in the chapel that day. Away from the intense negativity of the wing, I was suddenly reminded that peace and calmness were even possible in the world.

Instead of being bombarded by a hundred people's aggressive voices all at once, all I could hear was my own, serene inner voice. This was the first time since that awful night that I had felt comfortable and safe enough to pay my respects to my victim properly, in my own way.

Although I was returned back to the wing after those few moments in the chapel, I felt it had been both constructive and a very kind gesture by the vicar to offer me the chance to reflect. For a few moments as I prayed, I had the first clear sight of what the future might look like: a place where I might acknowledge my crime and be less angry with life. While I wasn't quite ready to fully immerse myself in that kind of thinking, and was quickly back in the negative culture of the prison wing, it did at least offer me hope that perhaps there was a better life for me after my sentence.

Frustratingly, there was a setback near the end of my sentence, when some individuals from The Meadows area appeared on other wings. I remember one occasion when one of them, who knew all about the beef between me and the friend who had snitched on me, was shouting, 'Hey Jacob, he's fucking laughing about it all on the outside and nobody is doing anything about it,' across the prison block.

Now, this information may not have been strictly true, because, first, this guy on the other wing was well known for being the type of nutter who liked to manipulate people and to stir the pot wherever he possibly could. And, second, my friend who had snitched had sent me a letter recently saying, basically, that he was sorry for everything but had now sorted his life out. 'I just fucked up. I didn't know what I was doing,' he said.

It therefore seemed unlikely to me that he was out there shouting his mouth off and laughing about my plight. In no way did I accept this apology when I read it, however. I simply wasn't ready to. And after I showed it to other friends in prison, I accepted it even less. Their reaction just riled me further. 'He fucking snitched on you,' they said. 'You've got to get even.'

Obviously these were entirely the wrong types of people to show an apology letter from a snitch, given that they were only ever going to reinforce my enraged view and then egg me on to exact some sort of revenge when I got out.

Again, the negative viewpoints I had acquired before going into prison were merely being reinforced on the inside. I was learning that in gang culture and in prison, no matter how independently minded you think you are, the mindset of those you surround yourself with definitely rubs off on you.

So, instead of feeling any better in myself, or especially sympathetic to my friend (I didn't write back, by the way), I found myself thinking, 'Well I'm glad you've got your life sorted out. I'm in here, with my mum going off her head on the outside and my life ruined, and you think a simple sorry is going to fix everything? Fuck that.'

Shortly before my release, the resettlement team, as it's called, came to ask me about where I was planning to go when I got out. Honestly, I had no real plan or means, but one thing I knew for sure was that I didn't want to move back into my mum's house. I made this very clear to both the prison and probation services, which would be dealing with me upon my release.

I had two reasons to think this way and the first was the most obvious: my mum had been completely out of control when I was in prison. As much as I was sympathetic and understood her problems, I just didn't want to put myself back into that toxic situation. Having been in prison for over a year, I couldn't see how that wouldn't be a backwards step.

The second reason was that I realised that if I didn't find a place of my own now, it was going to be a long, hard road to ever securing any kind of independence.

Looking back, as good as self-sufficiency might have sounded in theory, I was a long way from it in practice when I was released from prison. After all, on the day I walked out, I did so with no bankcard, no bank account, no email address, no record of my national insurance number – not to mention multiple holes in my bloody shoes. When some of my friends came to meet me outside the prison gate upon my release on 31 December 2012 all I had in my pocket was £40.

As it turned out, these friends – who were a little younger and certainly not wealthy – had gone the extra mile for me. Not only were they there to greet me, but they had all chipped in to buy me a new pair of shoes, a pair of jeans and a hoodie – in addition to stumping up another hundred quid in cash to get me going in the real world. I couldn't believe their generosity.

As if that wasn't enough, they then took me straight for an all-you-can-eat Chinese buffet. While we sat and ate, one of my friends created a Twitter handle for me using the word 'free-man' in it because he thought that was the most appropriate.

Given what I'd been eating for the previous year and a bit, I gulped this Chinese down like I'd never seen food. Then they dropped me off at my probation office.

There I was, back on the outside for real. As I closed the car door, I vividly remember thinking the strangest of feelings: that I felt a little loved again. My fragile ego was that receptive to any kind of affirmation.

The appointment time with the probation officer, Wendy, had been pre-booked before I was even released. It was she who gave me my licence terms and agreement, in addition to setting out any conditions that were to be attached to my release.

In my case, there weren't too many. Because James's family wasn't from Nottingham, I didn't have any limitations as to where I could go in the city and I wasn't on a tag. But I did have to go and see Wendy every week.

In general terms, a probation officer is there to keep an eye on you to make sure you're adapting to life on the outside. In addition, they are there to help you with anything you need regarding housing, education, work and whatever else may be required to get you moving on in life as opposed to slipping back into a spiral of reoffending.

I can't speak for the intentions and abilities of all probation officers, but I can say that Wendy definitely did have my back, right from the start. When she saw the report on me that detailed some of the diagnoses I had received, she said she could relate to them because she herself had an autistic son.

I felt Wendy had taken my case for the right reasons, and from the beginning I thought she was someone I could talk to and be comfortable with. Because of that, she became a vitally important person in my life at a time when I had absolutely no support or direction.

For example, in the days immediately after my release, I was sleeping on various friends' sofas, given that I'd already made it very clear I wasn't moving back to my mum's place. But there was a problem: one of the conditions of my release was that I had to have a fixed address. If I didn't, I could technically be returned to prison. Fortunately, Wendy understood my position and it was she who ultimately helped me register as homeless at the housing office, after which I was added to a list waiting for a room to become available in a homeless hostel. I was assessed and banded by priority and had to 'bid' weekly on available social housing properties. In the meantime, after a week or so, I was placed in the young person's section of a Salvation Army hostel.

On the second night after my release, I went round to the house of the friend who had snitched on me, bristling with aggression. Luckily for him, he wasn't there, but I got hold of him on the phone and found out that he was in Leeds for New Year. I planned to catch up with him when he was back, intent on resolving our beef one way or another.

Meanwhile, I went to see my mum for the first time since my release. She was obviously still struggling, but was clearly doing her best to give the impression she was coping okay. The house she was renting was mostly clean and tidy, she'd made an effort to get nicely dressed, and so forth.

My overriding memory of that reunion is of just feeling so guilty about everything.

Standing there in front of her, I gave her a big hug. It seemed entirely natural to do so. Then, not really knowing what to do with myself next, I walked into the kitchen and started washing the pots and pans that were sitting at the side of the sink – something I'd rarely done in all the years in which I'd taken her for granted.

'Aw, don't worry about that,' she said.

I wasn't quite sure how she took that helpful gesture of my mine – which I'm sure came as quite a surprise. As I said, she had clearly made an effort to make it look as if she had things together at home, so the last thing I wanted her to feel was that I was simply walking in there after more than a year in prison and highlighting the first job I saw that needed doing. No, I wanted to show her that I was a different and more considerate person by doing something that I had rarely done previously. It was my way of saying 'Sorry, I'm trying to change.'

As I left my mum's house that first time headed for another night on a friend's sofa, I remember feeling highly conflicted. All sorts of thoughts were flying around my head, and none of them sat very comfortably together.

First, seeing my mum had brought back all the guilt about what I'd done and what I'd put my already-struggling family through. A massive part of me wanted never to subject them to such heartache again and – by turning my life around – I really longed to make amends for the pain I'd caused.

But at the same time there I was going around the estate, nursing my hurt pride and brooding about how to reclaim it, a day or so after being released from prison for manslaughter. Although I felt some degree of contrition for my crime, I clearly wasn't yet equipped with the self-protecting instincts to reject the law of the streets – and that said my friend was a snitch and snitching on your friends should come at a heavy price.

Up to that point there had been absolutely no room for ambiguity on this issue. You either snitched or you didn't. The negative morality of snitching had always seemed obvious – at least in the criminal world I'd been part of.

Now, though, here I was with a criminal record, faced with having to reconcile this gang-culture code of honour with the law and the possibility of falling foul of it again.

I knew I had to choose, but I couldn't. So, in those initial moments of mental conflict, I did what I always did in such situations and pushed the thoughts away because I didn't know how to process them at that time.

As it turned out, I did go to meet my snitch friend a few days later and I did exact some form of revenge. I didn't physically assault him, as had been my intention for over a year. Instead, I

Jacob Dunne

made it perfectly clear some sort of reparation was needed and he paid me two and a half grand in cash from the proceeds of his job, in regular instalments over the next few months.

Did I feel good about committing what was essentially extortion? No, not particularly. One day if I'm wealthy enough I'll try to donate the equivalent amount to charity. But at least, in the end, the more rational side of my thinking had won over. I wanted to batter him, but I didn't want to go back to prison. So I tried to make him see everything from my position. I said 'Look, you've got a job; your life is fine. Meanwhile I'm on my fucking arse and I've got a criminal record.'

I actually feel he was sympathetic to my state of affairs. We had been very good friends, after all. Furthermore, I don't think he agreed to pay me because he was intimidated. He did it, I believe, because he genuinely felt guilty.

But for me the payment was an absolute bloody godsend. Because I had no job and no immediate means of earning any income, the three hundred quid he agreed to pay me at the end of each month became essentially a wage that really helped me find my feet in these difficult early days of freedom. Better still, it felt like I had also found a compromise position – albeit a shady one – between the gang code of honour and the law of the land.

Those first few weeks after my release were strange because I didn't feel like I had any particular purpose, especially when compared to the mind-numbing regularity of life in prison. I'd come out of prison with no qualifications, no fixed address, no hope or prospects.

So I did what I'd always done prior to my spell inside: I went back and forwards to my mum's, hung around with friends – many of whom were younger – and benefited hugely from the hospitality of their parents, who didn't seem to have a problem with me being an extra member of the family for a couple of days each week. Basically, it was business as usual, except that I was now an ex-con. I felt doomed to a life of crime. I had a label: I was a violent person.

Having said that, I do remember feeling curious about what people's opinion of me was now that I'd been in prison. Even then, with what was left of my dignity stripped away by incarceration, I still cared.

Why did I care?

Well, in prison, because you're in close proximity with cellmates for almost every hour of the day, you become very tuned in to people's moods and anxieties in a way that you just can't on the outside. Over time, I became more adept at reading people's thoughts based only on their body language and the nuances of what they were saying.

Given what I'd heard from friends, I knew that some people around the estate had been thinking, 'What's Jacob going to be like when he gets out?'

And in those initial days and weeks of freedom, I could definitely sense that kind of anxiety and uncertainty in a lot of the people who were around me. I could tell that they weren't quite sure whether I'd be approachable or aggressive. As it turned out, it seemed that people respected me more now that I'd been incarcerated, and I can't deny that felt good.

But I couldn't escape the reality that my position in the outside world was a perilous one. Although I had a helpful retainer from my snitch friend's wages, I still didn't have anywhere to live or any kind of long-term plan.

After a few weeks, I got word that a room had come up in a homeless hostel. Nothing about this place appealed to me, other than that there was breakfast available every day. I never once at there.

As snobbish as it might sound, I didn't want to be in close proximity to a load of homeless people, even though my rent was being paid for me. I didn't feel like I belonged there, despite all the facts saying otherwise. As a compromise, I stayed four nights a week so that I wouldn't lose my place, and continued to sleep on friends' sofas and do nothing of consequence during the first months of 2013.

By February, while nothing had changed in terms of my ambitions, my financial status had at least improved courtesy of a piecemeal collection of income streams comprised of money from my mate, disability benefits because of my mental health conditions and, finally, dole money.

Given that I was paying no rent in the hostel, I was probably walking around with eight hundred quid a month in my pocket, which, with few expenses to speak of, was quite a tidy sum for a 21-year-old.

Even when I got a flat in The Meadows in March of that same year, I was eligible for full housing benefit until I entered employment because I was classed as Band 2 (young person).

All told, life was now a lot less stressful. But I wasn't exactly plotting out a productive career path for myself. Instead, I could feel myself slowly getting sucked back into the inert lifestyle I'd followed prior to going to prison.

As far as I was concerned, rather than rehabilitating me in any meaningful way, being in prison had only reinforced the negative views of both the world and myself that I'd been cultivating since youth. To put it more generally, it was dawning on me that the prison system only teaches you to become a good prisoner, not necessarily a good person. Other than a very brief ARV (Alcohol Related Violence) Course, being in prison barely even paid lip service to the concept of rehabilitation. No wonder so many young people from areas like The Meadows reoffend fairly soon after leaving prison. The question was: would I become another statistic? The odds were certainly stacked against me.

Chapter six

Rehabilitation

It would be no exaggeration to say that the course of my young life completely changed at one of my routine weekly probation meetings with Wendy.

She began to tell me about a concept called 'restorative justice', where victims and perpetrators of crime, supported by trained practitioners, are brought together to express the harm caused by the crime and to establish what positive outcome might be possible moving forward. 'Remedi,' she continued, 'a restorative justice organisation, have been in touch. The parents of the man you killed want to ask you some questions.'

Apparently, David and Joan Hodgkinson had been unhappy about the length of my sentence and had unsuccessfully appealed for a longer one within the scope of the guidelines.

When that appeal didn't amount to anything and my release became imminent, I'm told they started looking for other alternatives by which to secure some of the basic answers that data protection made impossible for them to get without my permission/involvement.

It was then that the idea of restorative justice was mentioned to them, though I believe it was couched in a way that suggested that, because I'd already been released from prison, there would be no particular incentive for me to engage at all and therefore they should not expect much. Any restorative justice case has to be entered into voluntarily from both sides. It can't be imposed or used as a punitive tool.

To be honest, when the idea was first put to me, I was very much in two minds. Part of me felt, 'No way am I doing this!' Another part, that this could be my salvation.

I wasn't capable of making a decision right away. Instead, I went off to think about it, first by researching a little what restorative justice even was. I'd never even heard of the term until Wendy mentioned it.

What I discovered was that, though they were still few and far between, scenarios in which victims of crimes meet with the perpetrators were slowly becoming more common –the idea being to arrive at some kind of mutual resolution. In 2013, it certainly wasn't the law that all victims had to be offered this opportunity; it was merely a government guideline – and it was a service that had to be funded separately, in this case by a charity.

When I thought about the concept rationally, removing my own emotions from the equation, I could see how it made sense. Restorative justice gave victims some kind of voice. Given that the police, court and prison system had traditionally been focused on dealing with the perpetrators of crime rather than the victims, it was clear that the victims had always been a little neglected. I got it, but the million-dollar question remained: did I want to be part of it?

After a bit of soul searching, I made up my mind. Or rather, a combination of guilt and shame made it up for me.

A week later, at our next probation meeting, I walked straight in and told Wendy that I was willing to take part in the restorative justice idea – a process that is initially handled by practitioners who go back and forth between victims and perpetrators, carefully and sensitively relaying messages.

In my case, James's parents, David and Joan, were asked to compose a list of questions they wanted to ask me to start the dialogue. These were then relayed to me, whereupon I had the chance to give my answers before they were returned to them, and so on.

This arm's-length process was intentionally slow-moving and was handled by experts in mediating cases with sensitive subject matters, such as where a death occurred. From memory, the initial stage of the conversation went on for six to nine months, almost until the end of 2013.

David and Joan's questions at the beginning were unnervingly stark in their simplicity, and I honestly can't blame them for being so direct.

'Why did you do it?'

'Did James spill your drink?'

'Did he chat up a girl you were with?'

Then they asked what I thought was a strange question.

'Do you have martial arts or boxing training?'

In response to these questions, I gave David and Joan the absolute facts – that I was simply backing up my friends because they'd called me and that their son had done absolutely nothing wrong that night.

There was no argument, no drink spilled and certainly no girl. And I had no martial arts or boxing training whatsoever. All I had was a few years of street-fighting experience during which I'd been punched and been punched many times.

The truth was what they wanted, but I felt that the truth I was giving them was the worst kind – in the sense that it confirmed to them that their son had lost his life to a random act committed on the spur of a moment rather than anything premeditated.

In short, what I was saying was that I didn't know why I did what I did that night – and that I didn't even know why my friends had been arguing with their son in the first place. In every sense James Hodgkinson's death did not need to happen. It was shallow and, worst of all, unprovoked.

The simplicity of this truth must have been incredibly hard for David and Joan to comprehend, but it was also difficult for me to come to terms with, albeit on a vastly lesser scale.

Going through the beginnings of the process made me realise that the only way perpetrators like me can ever fully understand the absolute heartache and torment their actions have on their victims and loved ones is by entering into some kind of dialogue, regardless of how difficult that process is for both parties.

In my situation, as the initial rapport between us developed over these early months, I increasingly started to feel that to give David and Joan this information was the absolute least I could do. The shame and the guilt I felt every day made that so.

Furthermore, it's important for me to say that in no way did any of this dialogue lift the weight off my shoulders and that was never my intention. All these conversations did was humanise James and his parents further. In my position of detachment, I badly needed that to happen. Instead of being just names and pictures in a newspaper, when David and Joan told me about themselves, what kind of person their son was and what he liked to do, they all became human beings with lives and feelings.

Once I had this information and clear, indelible pictures had been created in my mind, I couldn't just push everything away and forget about it, as had been my way with anything I didn't want to deal with in the past. Now I was forced to confront what I had done and begin the unfamiliar process of accountability. With hindsight, restorative justice was probably the only way I would ever have done it.

In my eyes, it was an entirely one-sided process. The way I saw things, I was guilty and, as such, deserved no relief from whatever relatively inconsequential degree of mental torment I was going through. I was entirely focused on David and Joan and giving them what they needed, albeit that everything I did and said was underpinned by this horrible, hopeless knowledge that, although I wished more than anything that they could, my words would never bring James back for them.

Now that I'd taken the first step towards understanding my crime, I found it incredibly hard to live with the cold reality of what I'd done. But as difficult as the process was and as shameful as it made me feel, I stuck with it. I had no choice. I couldn't go back.

At the beginning, my only expectation from the restorative justice process was that I'd at least be able to answer the questions that David and Joan had about why their son had died.

Did I think I was going to change my ways as a result of the process? I'm not sure that possibility even entered my mind.

By this time l was living in the one-bed maisonette flat in The Meadows that Wendy had by this time helped me find. And during those initial months of mediation I had independently started thinking that maybe there was more for me in life than unsatisfactory jobs and low-level crime and/or drug dealing.

I didn't exactly know what it was that I was going to do long term, but a new willingness was certainly there, largely motivated by seeing other friends without a criminal past getting on in life, having relationships and families, and leaving criminality behind.

I'd also recently started in a new relationship myself, with a respiratory nurse I'd met on a night out in the city centre.

The girl was from Nottingham and had just finished at the prestigious University of Nottingham Medical School when I first ran into her. Our eyes met in a nightclub, we got along really well and exchanged phone numbers, then the next day I called her and we got together.

I can't remember when I told her about the more serious matter of my past, but I think we went on a few dates before I mentioned I'd recently been released from prison.

Looking back, I didn't want to hide the information at all. I just wanted to find the right moment to raise such a delicate subject. In fact, given that I'd already established dialogue with David and Joan, I think I actively wanted to explain my situation more.

By and large, I was finding that the very act of engaging in restorative justice was already helping me in the sense that it made me feel slightly less guilty, and therefore much more forth-coming when it came to discussing my past with anyone. Although I never said it, I wanted people to get the message: 'this is what I did, but this is what I'm doing to make amends'

This was the first stable relationship I had ever been in and I found the routine of spending time with someone who was working shifts helpful. The discipline needed meant we took turns to cook dinner to fit in with each other's working day. I was also able to pay my share of bills and such like, my mum having recently helped me get an occasional job putting up shop-front signage with a guy she'd gone to school with years back.

Next door to the signage company was a removal business, and before long the manager asked me if I'd help him out also whenever he needed a spare pair of hands.

The nature of this job – one in which I could show up a bit tired or hung-over – was perfect for me at that point in my life. Hard work though it was moving sofas and carrying wardrobes up three flights of bloody stairs, the job was positive because it also kept me in a routine where I had to show up for a job at a specific time. Not just that, it was initially cash in hand. I would do this removal job on and off for the next four years, and I would like to thank all those I worked with for the laughs and work ethic we shared as well as for putting up with me.

Simultaneously, and totally out of the blue, David and Joan started extending the scope of their questions at a point where I thought our dialogue was almost over.

Instead of asking for more explanations about what I'd done, they turned the spotlight back on me by saying words to the effect of: 'So, what do you intend to do with your life from now on?'

Although it came as a surprise, I don't think this was an intentionally loaded question. I don't believe David and Joan just wanted me to tell them what they wanted to hear; presumably, something along the lines of, 'I'm going to turn my life around.'

For all I know, it might even have been the restorative justice mediation practitioners themselves who suggested David and Joan should ask me the question. Knowing what I know now, the question would certainly be in keeping with the restorative ethos. Either way, it really gave me pause to think at a moment when I was perhaps at my most vulnerable.

It turned out to be the right question at the right time. They had the answers they needed to aid their healing, and had helped me feel a sense of shame at the same time. We'd reached some degree of closure on that part of the process, even though the answer I'd given them was I thought so empty it made their son's death seem pointless.

Now, despite the emptiness, and to their huge credit, the dialogue was being steered in a direction that was more positive and hopeful for all of us. Unbelievably, they didn't just want to take their answers and walk off into the sunset while condemning me to a life of shame and guilt. They wanted to discover how we could all move forward in our respective ways.

David and Joan's question proved a real catalyst for me personally. It took me to a place whereby, at my next probation meeting with Wendy, I walked into her office and said to her with no preamble whatsoever, 'I'd like to do my GCSEs again.'

And that's what I did. I enrolled in college for the following September.

Meanwhile, in the background, my mum's response to the whole restorative justice approach was a confusing one. I was moving forward because of restorative justice; she was being left behind by it.

To this day, I have no real clue why she took it as badly as she did. Being deep in the grip of addiction, as she was by this time, can't have helped. What I do know is that she adored her children and had spent her entire life doing everything she could to protect them and provide for them. That was indisputable.

But now, fuelled by her own problems with alcohol addiction, I suspect that she saw the mediation process I was engaged in as a reflection of her own abilities as a mum. Although that view doesn't really make sense, I genuinely think she felt she had failed, whereas the reality was that it wasn't her who had let people down, but me.

I was determined to push forward despite her misgivings, and the first step was to appear in front of a glum-looking panel at the college and convince them that, despite my criminal record, my desire to take my exams again was real. This was easy to do. I was so positive and hopeful. I didn't have to pretend.

In September 2013 I started an access to further education course, which included GCSEs in Maths, English and Psychology. At the beginning I wouldn't say that I had the best attitude to learning – mainly because of the scars left by the struggles I'd had in the past. But what was different this time was my willingness to work and my belief that, for once in my life, I was doing the right thing.

Not only that: at college, I also ran into a teacher who really knew how to motivate me. His name was Derek and I believe he was ex-military. Whatever he was, his GCSE Psychology course worked for me. He was tough and in fact some people were actually quite intimidated by him.

For me, his approach couldn't have been better. Unlike almost every teacher I'd ever encountered at secondary school, Derek was consistent to a fault. Consistent in his high expectations of me and consistent in his support. No matter how unforgiving his methods might have seemed at the time, I now fully understand from studies into restorative practices that he treated me like an adult rather than a problem child.

Instead of being scared of him like everyone else seemed to be, I actually enjoyed Derek's approach – mainly because I knew that, for all that his attitude to teaching was a bit hard-line because of his army background, he'd make me be accountable and keep me focused. More than anything, because he treated me the way he did, for the first time I found myself caring what a teacher thought of me as opposed to saying, 'I'm not bothered' and checking out.

So, for all that I threw myself into the process of passing my GCSEs for my own reasons, Derek deserves much credit in the story for unlocking the potential I perhaps always had.

Furthermore, because of him, and in spite of the legacy of the various diagnoses that had hampered me throughout secondary school, I was now more optimistic of trying in education – despite my limited belief in my capacity to learn.

I'm not totally sure what else fostered this newfound belief. After all, it had only been a few years since I'd been in secondary school and had failed spectacularly, rebelling to the point that I couldn't stay there. Prison, though, had shown me where I didn't want to be. Not only that; having been around enough people while I was inside to see how easy it is to embark on an endless cycle of reoffending and incarceration, perhaps I subconsciously felt that education was not just my best option in terms of improving myself, but also the only viable means I had to stop myself following that same cycle. Whatever it was, I knew that a change had started. I couldn't give up. I had to go all the way.

What made this change of attitude more remarkable was that outside of school my social circles and activities hadn't really changed much. While some of my friends had moved on with their lives, some hadn't.

Indeed, of the group I was socialising with on the weekends when I wasn't at college, a significant number of them just saw my attempts to re-educate myself as bloody stupid. There were very few I could talk to about why I was doing what I was doing. They just weren't in the same place of relative enlightenment that I'd reached.

'Why the fuck are you back at college?' they'd ask.

'I just want to finally get my GCSEs,' I'd tell them.

'Fucking hell,' they'd say. 'Good luck with that, mate.'

Despite this awkward position, I more or less held it together. I was doing 'adult' things such as redecorating my flat and getting a friend to help me replaster the walls. But I was still going drinking at the weekends and taking cocaine from time to time.

The way I justified the latter was by telling myself that such activities were now just harmless fun, and solely a means of offsetting what I was doing during the week. 'You're simply living a student life,' I told myself whenever the doubts crept in, suggesting that I should be living as a paragon of virtue 24/7.

Here's the hard part to admit, though. Even after having been in jail for causing someone's death in a late-night drunken altercation, situations did arise after I'd been released where I could easily have found myself in exactly the same place all over again.

It's not that I ever got into a fight with the aim of really hurting anyone. That had never been the aim of the many drunken scuffles I got involved in – and that includes the awful night when my actions ended James Hodgkinson's life.

As hard as some may find it to believe, given I was perpetrating an undeniably violent act by throwing a punch, I didn't intend to hurt him that night. My group's honour was under threat, along with my credibility as part of it, and the sad truth is that James – in his capacity as the symbol of that threat – was a random participant who just happened to be in the way.

After my release, similar situations frequently arose again, and in most cases my friends would be phoning each other for backup when things kicked off, as they always did. What had changed, though, in the aftermath of my prison term, was my personal role in such proceedings. Restorative justice had taught me something about mediation and, when it came to street-fight situations, the power of peacekeeping rather than blind conflict.

Whenever things got a bit out of hand at the end of a night out and it looked as though things might turn nasty I either slid off altogether, or stayed and played the role of a de facto mediator among my mates. I wasn't analysing this role too much; I certainly wasn't thinking, 'If I you don't do this, Jacob, there's a chance you could end up in prison again.'

No, I really believe I had grown up a little, and had come to an understanding that there is a better way than ego-driven violence – all of which I tried to make perfectly clear to my friends before we went out. 'I'm not here to get into pointless arguments over nothing,' I told them. 'I want to actually enjoy myself. So don't

expect me to help you if you get into any trouble. It's not worth it and I don't want to be around it.'

A week before I got my GCSE results (all 'A stars') in May 2014, my mum passed away. She was only 48. This made the following week so agonisingly bittersweet. Obviously, I was delighted that I'd succeeded at something for once, but at the same time I was devastated. I remember reading a poem I'd written for her funeral, with tears rolling down my face, heartbroken that my mum would never be able to witness that I'd really meant what I had been saying about straightening my life out.

Her death was all made worse by the fact that she had always believed in me, not only while I was at school and in prison, but equally afterwards. Never once did she stop trusting that I'd pull through and make something of my life. But then, at the moment when I most wanted her to see that her faith in me had been justified, she was gone.

The only solace I could take from my mum's death was that at least she had been there to see the change starting. And to this day, the idea of doing my mum proud has kept me going through some incredibly difficult times.

I wrote a poem a couple of nights before the funeral in one ten-minute tearful sitting. Whenever I have written in a time of need, I have felt better.

Faithful Journey

Mum,
Journeys start and journeys end
Journeys twist and journeys blend

Right From Wrong

> *Journeys' roads promise ups and downs, through dark*
> *through light through fog or rain, it's like the people on*
> *those journeys that make them change.*
> *I once walked a path that brought you worry and stress. It's*
> *hard to imagine how you managed the rest. Naïve, young*
> *and sometimes dumb, how lucky was I to have you mum.*
> *So here I stand, your son has grown, it's a credit to you I*
> *chose this road. The laughs, the smiles, the hugs, the*
> *trips, just some of many that I will always miss.*
> *You've done your job and man I'm proud, two sons you*
> *raised from just a child. If one thing's clear our future*
> *is bright, I know you will help and guide us right.*

The weeks and months following my mum's death were certainly some of the more difficult times, not least because my younger brother, Sam, now had nowhere to live.

In 2014, he was only 15 or 16 and was still doing his own GCSEs. The last thing he needed was further major upheaval at such an important time in his education. Sam, like me, was not enjoying school at all and was getting no help from any of the teachers whatsoever.

I remember discussing with Sam how school was going in the months before and after my mum's death. Often, we sat in the flat at night talking about the approaches these teachers took. For me it was like déjà vu.

'They think they can fix me,' Sam used to say. 'They say they want to help but they just give up as soon as I don't engage or try. So what's the point?'

I just thought, 'Hmm, that sounds familiar.' There was little I could do to help other than trying to set him a decent example, given that now we were both doing our GCSEs, and I was seven years his senior.

My dad came down from Manchester after my mum's death to talk to social services about where Sam should live. In the end it was a straight choice between living with me – in which case I'm sure Sam thought he would have fewer rules and restrictions while continuing to live in the only neighbourhood he'd ever known – or moving up north with our estranged dad, almost certainly getting less freedom and in an unfamiliar town too.

Really it was a no-brainer, so Sam moved in with me (along with my mum's dog). That brought home to me something my mum always used to say when she was alive: 'When I'm dead and gone, you two will only have each other.' Now we really did only have just that – and a lot bloody sooner than we thought we would too.

The time with Sam in the flat was difficult in that it made me (and him to a lesser extent) grow up so fast. On the other hand, I had no choice but to rise to the challenge and take on the responsibility, and it gave me another reason to continue down the positive path I'd set out on when I agreed to take part in restorative justice.

Just for myself, a relapse into crime and a return to prison would have been bad enough. But the predicament it would have left my younger brother in would have been unthinkable. No way was I letting myself, or Sam, down. As my mum also always used to say: 'You must always try your best.' And I did, while imagining that she was looking down on me approvingly.

With no other alternative available, life soon settled down into some kind of routine, with Sam going to school and me working during the week, and with me going to college and partying at the weekends. Sam stayed alternately at my aunty Julie and uncle John's houses with his cousins at the weekends (they had divorced not long before) and during the week he would stay with my aunty Paula and Nan. All of them helped and supported him a lot.

As it turned out, as easy as it would have been for him to run wild with only his elder brother to keep tabs on him, Sam didn't at all. Not only did he have our mum's death to come to terms with, but being 15 at the time he also faced the pressures of GCSEs and thinking about life after school. On top of this, and unbeknownst to me, he was also in the process of coming out as a gay man.

Looking back on this period in our lives, I have no idea how we both got through it. We rarely discussed each other's problems. Instead, we just got on with life as best we could and our relationship became incredibly strong because of that, even though I know he rightly despised me on more than a few occasions. He found it hard at times to accept that I was his legal guardian and was therefore in a position of authority. It took us a year on the waiting list to get a two-bedroom property and at that point Sam didn't stay with family as much because he had his own room. But I know I drove him crazy when I came back with friends after a night out and 'partied' till the early hours downstairs. It wasn't respectful at all.

For the record, he passed his GCSEs and left his teenage problems behind. Any time I see Sam nowadays, I just can't help reminiscing about those days in the flat and thinking, 'I had no idea what you were going through. I'm so bloody proud of you!'

Chapter Seven

Meeting Joan
and David

With hindsight, I think I must have known that my GCSEs were my last throw of the dice. For that reason, I worked harder for them than I'd worked for anything in my life – and that includes the degree course I'd later complete. As young as I was, I had seen the other side of life – the one that offered no hope or positive future – and I didn't want to go back there.

I passed my GCSEs with the highest marks in the college. Up until then everything I'd done since leaving prison had been motivated only by hope.

I hoped going back to college might be worthwhile.

I hoped not making quite as much money from employment in the short term would be a sacrifice worth making in the long term.

All I had was hope – and it was a pretty vague feeling underpinned by no particular reasons to believe that it was justified.

But as soon as I got those GCSEs everything changed. Suddenly I had some serious confirmation of my worth to cling to. I could envisage myself being something more than I'd always thought I was. I vividly remember thinking, 'Wow! Those diagnoses really don't need to be a hindrance if I'm willing to try.'

Suddenly, overcoming my situation was a viable option. In an instant, all the self-doubt that had been instilled in me throughout my entire educational experience previously, lifted. All the reasons why I became disenfranchised and had beaten myself up mentally in the first place just disappeared. The narrative I'd written for myself – entirely dictated by past experiences, insecurities and feelings – became mine to control going forward. Something as simple as three 'A stars' at GCSE had short-circuited the narrative from being bleak to becoming potentially bright.

In the days and weeks that followed, I felt a snowball effect take over, the positive momentum of self-confidence propelling me towards better things. I stuck at study tasks longer, when previously I would have given up. I stayed on at work to finish a job, when previously I might have clocked off. Everything about my outlook improved. I was flying.

After being asked that question about my future plans by David and Joan, all I'd told them at the time was that I intended to go back to college to do my GCSEs. Although I didn't say it or perhaps even acknowledge it to myself at the time, there must have been a part of me thinking, 'Me just saying sorry isn't enough. I need to show you with my actions too.'

Because of the slow nature of the back-and-forth, the next thing I was able to tell them was that, not only had I done just that, but I'd also achieved excellent results in the process.

But what about the future? Before my mum passed, she had put me in touch with a man in her church who worked in the Youth Offending Team in Nottingham. Every council has one and they manage young people aged 10-17 entering the criminal justice system. Over the last few months while my mum was still alive, he had kept in touch with me from time to time, occasionally suggesting that I join the church and perhaps give some talks to young people about my experiences.

While I was doing my GCSEs I hadn't really considered whether sharing my experiences was something I wanted to do. But once I'd passed them and started feeling this rush of positivity, and despite the residual heartache caused by my mum's death, I started thinking that maybe I could offer young people some kind of insight into how a young, disillusioned life can be turned around. And I thought too that my experiences might be beneficial for professionals working with young people like myself.

So I said 'yes' to this man. I was so high on adrenaline that found myself agreeing to pretty much every speaking or training request at that time. Wherever I turned, I genuinely thought I could make a difference. Passionate as I was, though, about this new opportunity, at the same time the guilt I was still feeling was also part of the fuel mix.

Subconsciously, everything I did thereafter was designed to change how I viewed my narrative in my own head. The first talk I gave was to share my story of restorative justice with a group of twenty or so community panel members, comprised of some older people like retired teachers, but also some students who were studying for a Criminology degree or such like.

I showed up, absolutely shitting myself with nerves, with these little cue cards that my former English teacher at college had shown me how to make, and gave this talk. I was shaking so much that I couldn't stand up. I had to sit down to finish.

However, despite my fears and total inexperience, the speech apparently went well, and because it did, one of the people on the panel – a guy called Hugh Shiel, who had connections at the Nottingham Youth Offending Team – asked me if I'd like to come and speak at an annual conference a few weeks later.

He said that in addition to the obvious power of my story, he also saw something in me as a person, and explained that they wanted a guest speaker who was a 'real life' example of the benefits of restorative justice.

Again, I thought, 'Yes ... come on!'

I bought my first ever suit for that conference and I can't begin to explain how good I felt. I really thought I'd found my vocation in life and believed that a future in speaking at conferences and the like beckoned – even though they made me anonymous at the time and gave me a name badge that said 'Tony'.

A manager on the team called Shelley later wrote about me 'He showed an unusual gift for public speaking and struck just the right tone, to the extent that everyone wanted to speak to him afterwards, and even suggest him for future employment!'

In the audience that day was a guy called Shad Ali, who was on the other side of his own restorative justice experience. Shad had been the victim of a racially aggravated GBH attack in Nottingham and had needed facial reconstructive surgery as a result.

The perpetrator was sentenced to what's called an IPP (Imprisonment for Public Protection) sentence – where he couldn't be released, regardless of the length of his sentence, until the parole board decided it was safe for him to be reintroduced into society. It's a bit of a strange situation in the sense that you can be given a sentence that ultimately isn't worth the paper it's written on because, at the end of the day, whatever the judge said in court could later be overridden.

Consequently, there are countless people who get three-year sentences on IPP, who are still in prison 15 years later. Nowadays, that sentence has been abolished, yet people still remain in prison subject to it.

Apparently, the perpetrator in Shad's case wanted to take part in restorative justice, but because he was on an IPP he wasn't allowed to. So, Shad was out there talking about this situation for an organisation called the Forgiveness Project.

He was an extraordinary case study because, while he had corresponded with his perpetrator, he couldn't go and meet him face to face. So Shad was basically a campaigner, and he was using his ability to talk as a means not only to petition for his right to take part in restorative justice, but also to express his belief that the criminal justice system was not working very well in terms of helping victims or offenders.

Listening to Shad telling his story, I couldn't feel anything but empowered by both his passion and his compassion. He was the real deal in every sense. Equally, when he heard me talk, I think he felt that I had something about me, too.

Because we were both from Nottingham and from different sides of the restorative justice process, he and I gravitated together quickly. He became my first real mentor, later putting me in touch with the Forgiveness Project, with whom I'd ultimately do work for within their prison programme called RESTORE, with help from another close mentor, Sandra Barefoot.

Everything I did around this time seemed to connect me with someone new. Wherever I went I met somebody with whom my story resonated, and that in turn organically led to something else positive and another invite. All of this was part of the snowball effect that I described. Once it started, it never stopped. And it told me that people were generally receptive to a story like mine and wanted to help me tell it.

All of the work I was doing meant I began to feel that, in order to do the best work I could in terms of giving speeches and helping others, I had to have some kind of academic foundation to reinforce my lived experiences.

In isolation, I knew that my lived experiences were valuable. But in order to give them even more context I needed the information and data that a degree would provide in order to make my message more rounded and less emotionally driven. In short, I wanted a more rational, scientific approach to the problems of society, and I knew that I needed a degree to give me that kind of statistical knowledge and credibility.

In order to be eligible to read for a Criminology degree, however, I had to first undergo an access to higher education course (a course for mature students equivalent to A-Levels), which encompassed social sciences, at the same college where I'd done my GCSEs.

I started this access course – where I met countless people who later turned their lives around – in September 2014. It took a whole academic year to complete, and once I'd passed it I decided to apply to do a degree in Criminology at Nottingham Trent University, beginning in September 2015. I chose Nottingham Trent because it was local and because my brother was still living with me.

Some people think that psychology – an integral part of both courses – is all about mind reading and so forth, but that's not it at all. Studying psychology isn't going to make your assumptions any more accurate or enhance your gut feelings. But what it did give me was a better understanding of myself.

The world of psychology fascinated me right from the start. I just couldn't get enough of it. It wasn't about wishy-washy theories with no real-life applications. Quite the opposite: the course offered a host of insights that I could apply in my own life on an almost daily basis.

Pretty much the first topic was the concept of reconstructive memory, where, for example, people look at eyewitness testimony with regard to the legitimacy of police witness statements. We went on to look at prejudices and stereotyping, what constitutes them and where they originate. Finally, we dug into learning methods and habits, which led us to Pavlov's dog (classical conditioning) and other such experiments.

I remember one related incident at the time very clearly. I can't quite remember what I was doing in town, but I think I had to take some pictures to get processed in Boots on my way to college in the morning. I dropped them off and went to my psychology lecture, which happened to be on content-dependent memory; for example, when you forget what you went into the kitchen for, go back to the place where you first decided to go into the kitchen, and doing that triggers the memory of why you elected to go.

After the lesson, I went for my lunch at an art gallery in Nottingham that I walk past on the way to college, went back to college and finished the day, completely forgetting about my photos in Boots.

Then, on the way home, when I walked past where I had my lunch, the memory was triggered. I was ecstatic. I was jumping around like a kid – proper excited about the fact that I was able to apply something we'd discussed in class that morning in real life later the same day. As I walked home, with my photos in hand, I thought, 'This is learning ...'

I also studied sociology, which – in conjunction with my access to further education course – helped me realise that the human mind and the environments it is exposed to make it susceptible to so many variables. I hope this understanding made me less judgemental in the sense that I had a greater understanding of how other people view the world in the way they do.

My girlfriend, meanwhile, had moved out during my access course and gone back to live with her parents. We didn't have a falling out per se, but I think it was pretty clear to her that, in addition to the flat being small for three people and a dog, I also had so much on my plate that I didn't have much bandwidth left for a serious relationship. We parted ways with no bad blood whatsoever.

Just before I started university in September 2015, my brother and I had moved out of the tiny flat in The Meadows and into the two-bedroom housing association place I was living in until recently.

By this time it had become clear to me that Sam and I had taken our mum's death in completely different ways.

For me, I just wanted to block everything out by partying with my friends when I wasn't studying or working. But perhaps because he was younger and didn't have the same number of social outlets I had, Sam seemed to keep himself to himself.

Extreme partying with lads I'd known for years was the path of least resistance for me. I managed to play two drastically different roles. I found support having a good time in the company of friends I'd known for so long, while at the same time enjoying much more meaningful academic conversations with teachers at colleges, engaging with people at youth offending conferences and guest lecturing – including at Cambridge University.

When I told my friends that one, they couldn't believe it. 'You serious, man? What was it like?' they said.

While not all of my friends could relate to everything I was now doing, if I managed to engage their imaginations they were soon interested. I set the scene, gave them a sense of the people and the atmosphere in the room – what it felt like the second I opened my mouth and projected my voice across the audience as my heart pounded with nervous energy.

I think the reason they got it was that we were all gamers at heart. Anything that was a little 'out there' tickled our imaginations and got us excited, and I found that I could use even the basics of what I'd learned in my psychology classes to make conversations with my friends exciting enough to draw them in. So we were still able to relate to each other, even while our paths in life were clearly diverging.

Although getting off my head with my friends was my way of blocking out Mum's death, it didn't always work. Although things were going relatively well in my professional life on the back of my good exam results and the connections I'd made in the community, there was always this shadow looming over me that I never fully addressed.

The truth is that, because I was so focused on trying to better myself and help others, I never truly developed the capacity to grieve for my own mum. I'm not even sure that I have done so today. I thought about her of course. How could I not? But rather than process the feelings, I pushed them away for another day. I knew that I needed help, but I didn't want to either tell people or admit to myself that I wasn't feeling great. I was worried that the very state of needing help meant that my rehabilitation had failed somewhat.

I think this seed had been planted me in when I first went to be interviewed to join the community panel for my local youth offending team. In the interview, I was asked directly if I'd ever had any 'help', and at that moment I said 'no', which was true. They didn't admit me to the panel. Instead they sent me away, saying something along the lines of, 'Let's see where you are in a year or so and we will reconsider ...'

However, I'm nothing if not an over-thinker and just a little paranoid, so before long I had that innocent question of theirs twisted around in my head to the point that I thought they were implying I was faking everything, and wasn't therefore as able and trustworthy as I was making out.

What I didn't know at the time was that there's 'something wrong', to some extent at least, for pretty much everyone. Whether you're the prime minister, a footballer or a bin man, there are days when you don't feel well and there is absolutely nothing wrong with that. It doesn't make us lesser, and it certainly doesn't invalidate other progress. It doesn't help anyone to hide it either. But for me, because of the trajectory I'd been on, it felt like there was a massive stigma attached to having the odd bad day. It was just one more way in which I was putting massive pressure on myself to not fail in any way. It took me a long time to acknowledge that sadness and depression can be normal.

For Sam things were different, as I only found out later. While I feel as though I didn't do much to support him in the weeks and months after Mum's death, through the vicar at St George's Church, which my mum and Nan still attended, we secured him some bereavement counselling sessions in Leicester at an organisation for young people called the Laura Centre. I never once thought to arrange any similar sessions for myself.

From what he's told me, the counselling really helped him. Our mum's death was magnified for him by the fact that he was already in a private torment of his own related to his sexuality – a subject that he certainly didn't feel comfortable enough to discuss with his older brother at the time. I don't think that was because he thought I'd judge him or not understand; I just think he saw that there was so much else going on in our world that his struggle with his sexuality would have only added to an already complex mix. Not only that, it now occurs to me that my super 'masculine' past might well have made me less approachable.

As it is, I've learned enough to understand that he and I are different people who process things in different ways. I did the best for him that I could in the aftermath of Mum's death and I'm grateful I had family and friends who could help us.

I was trying to be a parent while I was barely an adult myself. I have to give great credit to my nan, my auntys, Paula and Julie, and my uncle, John, who all picked up the slack where I couldn't.

When I received my degree offer I wrote to tell David and Joan the news, again through the mediation process. This letter was no different from the other two or three we'd exchanged over the preceding 18 months. But something obviously changed in them when they heard I was taking this next step into education, and instead of simply wishing me well for my future and cutting ties altogether – which they absolutely would have been entitled to do – they suggested a meeting in person as the next step in our restorative process.

When I heard that David and Joan wanted to meet me, I can't say I was totally surprised. Part of me had long suspected the process was leading up to this point. In fact, when David and Joan were first asked if they'd consider meeting me in those early stages, they apparently responded by saying something like, 'Maybe in about ten years' time', which, ironically, is roughly the amount of time it has been to now, as I sit writing this book. It's entirely possible that they just threw that ten-year number out there in an attempt to kick the possibility down the road a little, in a 'we're not ready now, but maybe some time down the line we might be' sort of way.

Anyway, there we were, two and a half years later, contemplating a meeting. A lot had happened to me in that time, and most of it was positive. Rather than reoffending, as all statistics suggested I might, I'd made huge strides personally. And not only had I engaged with David and Joan respectfully through restorative justice, but I had also, in the few educational speeches I'd given about my crime, positioned their feelings and wishes at the absolute top of my priority list.

It was agreed by the mediators that we should meet on neutral territory – and that turned out be in a modern and fairly clinical community centre in Suffolk – a two-hour drive for me, and a one-hour drive for them.

I'm not ashamed to say that, on that morning of the meeting, I was a bloody wreck. Someone who worked for the charity picked me up and I remember feeling so incredibly nervous sitting in the car – but not so apprehensive that I wanted to hold up my hand, stop the car and back out of the arrangement altogether.

I knew I had no choice but to go through with this meeting. Part of me, I guess, thought that a face-to-face meeting would represent the moment when I'd done all that I possibly could to respect David and Joan's wishes. Beyond that, I hoped that meeting them in person would show them that I was a changed person who had learned from my mistakes.

We arrived what seemed like an hour in advance of them. In reality it was probably only five minutes. Nevertheless, I just sat there in this side room on the ground floor with my head in my hands and a cold sweat beading on my back.

At one point, I intuitively sensed that David and Joan had physically arrived in the building. I just knew.

The moments before we all met felt like I was standing at the access hatch in the side of an aeroplane at 30,000 feet with a parachute strapped to my back. No part of me wanted to jump, but every part of me knew I had no choice. I walked up the stairs a step or two behind the lady, and along the corridor to a door with a long but narrow window running down the side, which I was surprised to see was blanked out.

I remember thinking at the time that that was a good thing. If I'd walked through the door of the room and they'd already seen me through the window, that somehow would have made things harder.

I stared at the door handle for a few seconds, while it looked back at me as if to say, 'Come on …'

Holding my breath, I opened the door and walked into the room.

David and Joan gave me nowhere to hide and I don't blame them. They both stared directly at me as I moved across the room. After respectfully meeting their gaze, I instinctively reverted to what I knew. I put my head down to avoid further eye contact. I don't think I did this because I wanted to mentally check out on this occasion, as I had while standing in the dock in court. This time I think it was more because I wanted them to lead the social interaction and not me.

Nevertheless, they could tell I was nervous, so to my relief they stood up. We acknowledged each other, said hello, while the two practitioners who'd been with us throughout the entire process sat at either end of the table. David and Joan took their places opposite me.

I'd always had a sense that Joan was the easier of the two to communicate with. Indeed, throughout the mediation process, I'd got the impression that it was she who was 'talking' to me more than it was David. None of this is to say that David hasn't been anything other than courteous and responsive whenever we've been in touch. But he's always done so without ever being over-friendly – which I totally respect and understand.

Perhaps because David spends half the year abroad and is therefore less accessible than Joan, I was made aware that it was important for them both to revisit their loss now that I was sat in front of them. Only then did we move on to discuss my progress. As much as I thought I knew David and Joan because of the mediation process, it's obviously a different prospect entirely when you meet someone in the flesh. They turned out, though, to be more or less what I envisaged in my mind's eye. Whether I was what they expected me to be, I have no idea. All I know is that I went in there not just having written letters to them, but also having tangible achievements to point to that confirmed I wasn't just a fraud who'd been telling them what they wanted to hear. I really did feel contrition and wanted the best possible outcome for them in desperate circumstances.

At first, we went over some of the ground we'd covered in the earlier question-and-answer dialogue we'd had in writing. In those initial exchanges through the practitioners they were able to talk about the impact and consequences of my actions and it was important for them to be able to revisit this with me in person. In their own way, they expressed how they'd felt at the beginning, and then how things had progressed to the point that we were now in the same room together, looking at each other across a table.

Listening to this I can't deny that I felt extremely jittery and nervous, even though we'd discussed it all in writing and via mediation previously. At one point I lost it completely and felt my airway closing. I tried to get a glass of water and was spilling it all over the place as I tried to take a sip. I felt and probably looked extremely vulnerable sitting there, but maybe that reinforced their belief in me.

I felt even more vulnerable when they went on to tell me more about James, their son, as a person – that he was well liked, loved extreme sports and a bit of danger. When I was in prison it was easy for me to blank the thoughts out when all I had was a photograph image to go on. Now, there I was with this person's mum and dad sitting five feet away from me, telling me intimate details about their son's life and broken hopes. That was the toughest part of the whole process for me. It was incredibly courageous of David and Joan to be so open and expressive for the hour we were together.

Even better, not only did David and Joan see me as an authentic person who meant what I said, but they actually took things a step further by saying that they wanted to support me in whatever messages I planned to relay in future talks, speeches or in the media –not only about the fact that a single punch can kill, but also about the benefits of the restorative justice process for victims of crime.

To me, this endorsement meant everything. While the whole point of the process had been to allow David and Joan the opportunity to express how they felt and to encourage me to understand the tangible effect of my actions, the meeting was a weight off my shoulders because to that point I'd just been acting on trust. While it was obvious during the mediation process that our relationship was advancing, I needed the in-person contact to really confirm, from the horse's mouth, that they believed and trusted in me.

Once I saw it for myself, their belief in me fuelled my own self-confidence. Honestly, it would be no exaggeration to say that David and Joan saved me by giving me a second chance in life. To this day I'm in awe about how they turned their anger and heartache into any sort of compassion for me. The two people I'd harmed the most with my actions had judged me the least.

Even though I'll never be able to fully repay them, I wanted to honour their son's life by changing and setting a good example for others.

Chapter Eight

Reaching Out

When I left the meeting with David and Joan, I felt some degree of closure in the sense that the first chapter of our relationship – in which we'd forever be painfully entangled on some level – had at least been written, approved and signed off.

With a sense of inner satisfaction that came from having received their blessing, I embarked on my three-year-long degree course with the same kind of enthusiasm and sense of positive momentum that I'd been feeling prior to meeting them in person.

University was to prove as valuable to me as college had been in the sense that all the lecturers there reinforced positive values in me. I started to feel like a lump of Play-Doh to which everyone just kept adding another piece, so that a mass was gradually created that had even more uses. As this happened, I felt increasingly confident about myself and assured about what I could possibly achieve with my life. My accountability and persistence had given birth to a sense of agency, and a feeling that I could in fact determine my own life.

Alongside what was a pretty intensive degree course with many practical case studies along the way, I continued with my outreach work across the country, none of it for my own benefit, and again fuelled by contacts that I met while speaking at the various events I was invited to attend.

Unity Football Club was one such organisation keen for me to come along and share some positive messages. It had been set up to appeal to youngsters from different parts of Nottingham, with the primary aim being to discourage gang culture. I was certainly well aware of Unity throughout my late childhood and teenage years.

The guy who ran it, Morris Samuels, was well known to all my friends and me, given that he also worked as a nightclub doorman in the city centre from time to time. He invited me to speak at some of his community events to which they invited stakeholders for either pre-match or post-match talks. Morris had probably seen me speak at a previous Youth Offending Team meeting and it went from there.

From that point my community work snowballed further. I kept saying yes to all the people who approached me to do things for them. I went into schools, joined the youth-offending team some weekends – and spoke at a variety of events with organisations of all kinds in the Nottingham area.

Basically I became this go-to guy for resources for all the local restorative justice trainers. Facilitators used me to fill in half a day of their training session and I was very happy to do so. I'd speak to social workers who were being trained, community ambassadors, children's nurses – all sorts of people from all kinds of different places, alongside doing my first year at university.

That community work was heavily reliant on me sharing my story. Every time I stood up to talk in those early days, I felt as if I was rewriting my own narrative. You see, I believed that my story was the only resource I had, and, obviously, I gave that account many, many times. How many people tell their life story once, far less hundreds of times and in public and off the top of their head?

Regardless, I just went in, told my tale and hoped to stimulate some interesting questions afterwards. It was all good stuff; people wanted to hear it. But I began to realise that people wanted me to do more and were asking not just for me to fill in for half a day, but to book me for two or three days of work.

Obviously it felt good to be in demand, but at the same time I understood that a three-day appearance would require much more of me than an informal half-hour chat. The quality that had got me this far was my ability to conduct myself well when delivering talks or helping to train people – something I had become good at because of the intensity of the position I found myself in in the public eye. There I was, this young person who was raising my hand and saying not only that I'd killed someone, but also that, despite having only been out of prison for a couple of years, I was a changed man and had met the family of my victims.

I didn't realise this at the time, but as well as the role I'd claimed for myself coming with a huge amount of responsibility, that very responsibility gave me the confidence I needed to talk freely about any subject going forward.

Again, I was fine with the role evolving. But I also realised that I had little knowledge of the kinds of skills you might learn if you were studying a postgraduate course in teaching:

constructing a lesson, running a workshop, and so on. And let's face it, if I was being booked for a couple of days of work, I knew I had to be able to do these things in order to make the time engaging enough to keep a group interested. So I started developing such skills in combination with the studies I was doing in my second year at uni.

It wasn't until my resources expanded later that I was asked to talk to what I'd refer to as 'normal' kids. Instead, I was tasked with working with the most difficult individuals – the ones who were about to be excluded from school or who had already been put in a school designed for kids excluded from 'normal' schools.

These places weren't like any school I'd ever been in. They were basically prisons under another name, and their ingrained anti-establishment culture was no better than places like HMP Glen Parva, where I'd been incarcerated. I couldn't just walk through the doors of these schools; I needed a key fob to move through them.

The advantage I had walking in there was that I saw so much of my previous self in these troubled kids. I could tell what the culture of a place was very quickly. I knew they were probably already selling drugs. There was a fair chance they'd already been arrested a few times. As someone who's been in prison, you just know.

Beyond that, because of my lived experiences, I could walk into any room, scan the faces staring back at me, and immediately have a pretty good idea about how serious the group was in terms of their level of disillusionment. I could also tell how much pain they were in because of that. I'd seen it in my friends, family and people in the community I lived in. I'd felt it in myself and seen it in the mirror every morning for years.

Because it hadn't been that long since I'd been in the world these kids were now in, I was able to stand on the outside, with insider knowledge of the scene, and explore with them the potential impact of pointing out each other's insecurities and egging each other on.

'How is this serving you?' I'd ask. 'We should be being good friends and asking each other if we're actually okay.'

Consequently, they bought into me – or what I used to be – and my narrative to the extent that they saw me as a warning of what might happen to them if they continued down the path they were on. Not only that, they also saw me as someone who couldn't just be dismissed or disrespected like their teachers.

However, in situations where I was talking to groups of angry youngsters, I always felt as if I still had to answer a key question they'd be subconsciously asking, given my words and demeanour, and that was, 'Is he legitimately street enough?'

This was a difficult thing to show because, while I'd ingratiated myself with and proved myself to the lads I hung around with throughout my teenage years, in my younger years at school I had always felt that I wasn't legitimate.

So, in those first moments walking into the worst school environments, I attempted to present myself as being mildly hostile, simply to ensure that I received a basic level of respect right from the start. Fear, after all, is often the currency that underpins hierarchy and respect among such young people – in the same way as it plays a big role in prison hierarchy.

When you boil it down, the thing that really made me legitimately street in the slightly sick minds of young lads – probably as desensitised to violence as I was in my teens – was the fact that I'd been to prison because I'd killed somebody. Not exactly the kind of street cred you're proud of or would want to broadcast, but in these environments details of that kind actually counted for something.

Not only that; because I also had the snitching element to my story, I knew I had a serious hook to hang the narrative on. Because that narrative went straight to the core of street mentality and values, it would also be the easiest way to secure engagement from young people who were already sufficiently indoctrinated to believe in and live by the laws of the street. My view, incidentally, is that if young people are already indoctrinated with street values, we as a society have failed them.

Essentially, then, I thought on my feet and freestyled my talks to suit how far the kids in front of me had been sucked into street culture. Often I used the snitch angle upfront in my story because I knew how much it would resonate quickly and deeply. And I was right. As soon as I introduced it, many of these troubled kids bought into me as a person and into the narrative I was standing there telling them. It's important to befriend before you challenge.

In their heads, I guess their primary reason for investment was that they wanted to hear what happened to the snitch – preferably, that he ultimately paid some kind of terrible price.

But later I would blind-side them with the twist in the plot – that not only had I pushed back from the established rules of gang culture by forgiving the snitch, but I had also taken my rehabilitation further by connecting with the parents of my victim.

I could see the shock in their eyes as I made the big reveal. I doubt any of the kids saw that ending of the story coming – but because I'd hooked them by frontloading the talk with the elements I knew would interest them, they were forced to hear the whole message I was there to relay – and that was that gang mentality and the associated violence isn't the way forward.

I was fine with holding myself up as both a cautionary tale and an example of redemption. Just like everything in life, some got it and some didn't. As an educator, that's all you can hope for and expect. The way I saw it, I was at least planting seeds for those who didn't immediately get the point. Hopefully one day in the future it would make sense to them.

Now and again, I'd receive a message on social media after a talk or a session from someone who'd been there. A few would just say something appreciative, such as, 'Thanks for coming today', whereas others – including some kids' mums even – would say things like, 'Your words at assembly today really helped my son talk about certain things for the first time.' These were the moments of connection that I really held on to.

Another outcome I quietly hoped for in the aftermath of my mum's death was that some of these kids would, rather than battling with their parents every day, try to make more of an effort with their own families and those who had their best interests at heart. Not making more effort with my own mum is one of my biggest regrets.

At the beginning of year three, I knew I would have to take a more disciplined approach to the Criminology course, simply because it involved having to submit a lengthy and quite involved dissertation at the end of it all.

As my second year at university drew to a close I had already started questioning what I was doing on a couple of levels. First, as much as I was attempting to help young people in the community by sharing my story, how much of what I was doing was really helping them in real terms?

Let's face it, these things are incredibly hard to measure at the best of times, and it wasn't as though, after giving a half-hour talk to a group at a school assembly, I could go back a year later with a feedback form for them to fill in. These things just don't happen. The reality was that I'd probably never see any of those kids again. All I could do was hope that something I said stuck in their heads.

Second, given that my course had just one year left, I found myself realising I honestly didn't know what I wanted to do with it. Part of me wanted to go into probation work full-time, but that's as much thought as I gave it. I was under no particular pressure, so was happy to keep surfing the wave, finish the degree and see what was at the other end.

It was about that time that the first of a few media opportunities presented themselves. Again, I didn't go looking for them. I hadn't advertised myself or my services at all up until that point. Every referral had come because somebody heard me talk.

From memory, the first was a programme on ITV called *A Tonight Special: Meeting My Enemy*, in which David, Joan and I talked about restorative justice and how the process had not only helped us, but also created a bond between us on a human level.

We were one of two restorative justice cases highlighted on the show, the other being about a person who burgled an old lady's house and they ended up getting together to talk about the impact that crime had had. The cases were different, but the outcomes were similar.

As a promo to that documentary, Joan and I appeared on *This Morning* with Phillip Schofield and Holly Willoughby.

I can't deny that it was all a bit surreal to sit there on the *This Morning* sofa talking about restorative justice as the police mugshot of me taken on the day of my arrest flashed up on the screen. It all felt a world away from talking in some echoey school hall. I barely recognised the angry and confused young man in the mugshot. Sitting there in that interview reminded me of how I felt when I sat in front of David and Joan for the first time. My mouth was dry; I was shaking.

I could be wrong about this, but I definitely got the impression that the presenters wanted to go much harder on me when I was sat there in front of them than they had led me to expect in the lead-up to the programme. They probably looked at the details of the case, just like anyone else, and made a judgement based on that. But then, when they saw that I was actually genuine, someone who truly felt remorse and was trying to turn his life around, maybe that helped changed their view and, by extension, how they treated me on the show – which I thought was very fairly, by the way.

It's not for me to say of course, but I always got the impression that bringing my authentic self into whatever room I walked into was what brought out a sense of compassion in whoever I was in front of, whether that was Philip Schofield, university students, or a group of disenfranchised school kids from tough backgrounds like mine.

Just as I had to prove to tough kids that I was street enough to talk to them on their level, I also made it my business to demonstrate to mainstream media, and academic institutions such as Cambridge University and TEDx, that I wasn't a fraud and was doing everything for all the right reasons with a real desire to help people in situations similar to that I had once been in. I had to find that middle ground between being rough around the edges and being mildly media savvy.

To make that easier for myself, any time I talked to the media or indeed anyone else, I did so imagining that David and Joan were watching. I never wanted to say or do something that could be construed as being disrespectful in any way.

The TEDx talk I gave in Bath in 2016 was probably the culmination of my experiences speaking live to a large group of people. My invite to speak there only came about because Charlotte Calkin – who worked as a restorative justice trainer at the time – had seen Joan and I speak together at an AGM conference run by Remedi, the charity that took my case on in the first instance.

'I'm arranging this TEDx talk in Bath in a few months. I think it would be amazing if you'd consider speaking for us,' she told me.

From there we started talking, and Charlotte and I have been working together on restorative justice initiatives of various kinds ever since. She has become another important mentor for me.

The funny part about it is that Charlotte came and did a load of prep work with me before the talk, but as soon I got up there on stage, it all went out the window. I did everything off the cuff. I had cards in my hand but I might as well have thrown them away!

I humbly believe that TEDx was my best talk on camera. I've had other sessions that weren't on camera where I've left thinking, 'I think I did well in the sense that what I said was powerful and the room seemed to be with me every step of the way.'

I never thought this in an arrogant sense; it wasn't about me. But whenever I said something that I could see people were relating to and connecting with, it made me feel pleased that I'd achieved what I'd been asked to do. I got the sense that those I was working with were becoming able to reimagine themselves in different ways away from the clutches of fear.

Equally, whenever I gave a talk that elicited little back from the audience by way of interaction, the only person I blamed for that was me. Given everything I've experienced, the last thing I ever want to do is blame other people for anything. One of the things I vowed I'd do in life was to accept accountability at all times with no excuses – both for my positive traits and for my negative ones. Easier said than done, granted, but a good guiding star nevertheless.

To that extent, if an audience didn't engage, that was because I'd somehow failed to present my information in the right way. I knew I couldn't be accountable for how other people responded; I could only be accountable for how well I prepared and delivered. So instead of moping about it and stewing over indifferent sessions, I left on these occasions thinking: 'What does that say about me?' 'How can I be better?' 'What can I request from schools/ organisations to achieve this?'

TEDx Bath was one of those days when everything I'd been learning over the preceding three years came together. Somehow I found the right balance of being the lad from The Meadows who could talk the talk, and someone who had just enough polish from doing a few bits of media work to present another more redemptive side of the same coin. Having said that, I knew I was talking to sixth-form A-Level students and didn't have to try to be too 'street'.

Nevertheless, when I watch it back nowadays, which I don't enjoy doing, I can see how incredibly nervous and vulnerable

I was: I kept having to pause to draw breath; to mentally pinch myself that I was standing up on a stage with a large audience hanging on my every word.

But when I detach myself and think in terms of that person being a stranger I'm interested in listening to, I can see the authenticity in the awkward, faltering delivery. One of the unhelpful consequences of my ADHD is that my mind skips ahead of where I am – a position that inevitably trips me up at times.

I have always been very mindful of the fact that the subject matter of my talks is not something that could ever be discussed flippantly. A young person died because of me. To have been rushed and dismissive would not only have had less impact on the various audiences I was addressing, but in my mind it would have also have been disrespectful to David, Joan and James. I just can't talk to people about these subjects in anything other than a measured, deliberate way.

TEDx Bath taught me many things, but what I learned most is that it is absolutely fine to slow down and make one's delivery even more thoughtful and measured. As it happened, I stumbled upon this realisation by accident – even though people came up to me afterwards and said words to the effect of, 'I've never heard so much power in silence.'

I can't take any credit for this powerful silence, sadly. I hadn't intended to be slow and measured – that's just the way it came out because of the sheer gravity of how I was feeling up there. I wouldn't say I enjoyed it per se, but I'm proud that I was able to do it, especially given that I was swarmed by young lads and girls afterwards, all of whom were keen to tell me how much they wanted to do what I was doing.

Chapter Nine

The Compass of Shame

Towards the end of 2016, I started becoming aware of a strange paradox in my life, a thought kept coming back and back to me.

I knew that every talk I gave, every school I went into and every media appearance I accepted, all moved me further down the line of rehabilitation and personal growth. That was undoubtedly positive. But, at the same time, I also knew that the reason I was being invited to speak at these events was the power of my story — to the extent that one could not exist without the other.

And I couldn't help but wonder whether, still in my mid-twenties with a whole life ahead of me, I would ever be anything other than the protagonist in the story I was telling people. I realised that there were certain things I was agreeing to that were no longer helping me and, in some cases, were actually setting me back.

What I was wrestling with at that time were the closely interlinked concepts of shame and guilt – the two emotions that I now know had motivated me most in my decision to engage with David and Joan in the first instance. It was them who helped me to have faith in my attempts to change.

People often say, 'What's the difference between the two?' My understanding is that shame is something we ourselves and others attach to a bad act that has been committed. These feelings of shame and guilt are relational feelings – dependent on social exchanges between people to control behaviour and determine the parameters for what is deemed to be right and wrong. Socially we use shame to control unwanted behaviour. We make people doing 'bad things' feel like 'bad people' by giving them community service and highlighting their actions in the news. Through humiliation, punishment, stigmas and labels, we use shame as a societal tool.

While you are feeling shame, you are defined by your actions. However, it's not realistic or healthy to stay in that place of shame forever. At some point you have to move from shame to guilt – a position whereby you can distance yourself from your actions to the extent that you can say to yourself, 'I did a bad thing, but that doesn't make me a bad person.'

These are academic subjects. Endless theories exist concerning the concepts. The Compass of Shame is the best known, and I explored it and many others in my university degree dissertation.

Shame vs Guilt

This distinction between guilt and shame cultures may seem ambiguous, but theoretical developments have made important distinctions between shame and guilt. Shame elicits a response that leaves an individual feeling bad about themselves as a person, whereas guilt leaves an individual feeling bad about the act that produced the negative feeling.

For example, two people could behave in a way that either offends somebody, or falls short of a specific standard that is important to others. The response to not meeting these norms or ideals is where the difference between shame and guilt is defined. The individual who experienced guilt would feel bad about the behaviour, whereas the person who experienced shame would feel bad as a person.

It is this leap from doing something bad, to being someone bad, that many labelling theorists have studied. Dating back to Frank Tannenbaum's (1938) 'dramatisation of evil' hypothesis, which suggested that communities first define individual acts as evil, before eventually going on to define the individual as evil through attaching stigmas and stereotypes. Therefore, even the existence of contemporary labelling theories suggests that this transition from shame- to guilt-based cultures has not been smooth or straightforward, and is a transition that is still in process. However, the distinction between guilt plays an important part in healthily navigating shame, which previous narrative theory capitalises on to support people in externalising deviant labels from the self.

However, as helpful as theory is (self-esteem is closely inter-linked with feelings of shame), I also know that in practice it may not be so easy to separate what we have done from who we now are and the regard in which we hold ourselves.

In my case, before I went to prison, the way I dealt with the shame of being unable to learn in schools, feeling like I had to prove myself to mates, having no dad at home, and even having a slightly malformed breastbone, which meant I was reluctant to ever take my top off, was to take no responsibility, lash out, and blame other people and society generally for all the problems in my life. This led to me being impulsive, withdrawn and violent – and that downward spiral ultimately led to me going to prison. That was shame version A for me.

Version B is where I found myself in the years after I came out of prison, engaged in a restorative process and began helping others. Instead of outwardly wanting to hurt other people with my words or fists, I arrived at a place where, because of my low sense of self-worth, I turned the feelings of shame inwards to the point that I was harming my state of mind.

Some people might call that progress, and I suppose in a way it was, in the sense that I have never reoffended. But the downside was that although my relationships with others had improved massively, the relationship I had with myself was deteriorating. Internalising rather than expressing my shame was the lesser of two evils, even though I couldn't get away from the sense that feeling depressed represented failure. After all, I had it alright.

Because of this conflict, for the first time I started becoming even more aware of mental health issues of my own that I'd pushed away following the deaths of my mum, my nan and my friend Shad. I realised that the reason I was feeling depressed and anxious wasn't so much because I actively wanted to transcend my past, but more because I felt conflicted and guilty about even wanting to move on.

I was crippled by grief, and on top of that had not been clear with Jess about what my own boundaries were for this new relationship, what my expectations were going forward, and all the other things that help to build a solid clear foundation. I wasn't sure how exactly I was feeling. I had shut down, and remained in a state of overwhelm and depression for some time.

Does that sound complicated?

Well, it was. I wrestled with it constantly and it hampered every thought I ever had about what I wanted to do with my life when I left university. I went back and forth in my head with the dilemma for ages. One part of me thought that maybe I should just be happy to even have the life I had. The other part would kick in say, 'Yes, but should I really have to accept that I'll always be defined by one strand of my story and by one punch?'

There was no easy answer – so in the short term I didn't deal with it all and just let life sweep me along instead. In no way was this approach helpful, and it's a route that I believe causes many of today's mental health problems. Personally, in combination with every other emotion I was blocking out (grief, loss and so forth), I was quickly heading for a mid-life crisis in my mid-twenties.

People tend to think about a situation in just one dimension: 'This feels uncomfortable, therefore I don't want to deal with it right now.' Everybody does this, probably on multiple occasions every day. But what they don't realise is that by deferring addressing feelings and their root causes, they are only adding to the discomfort and making it greater when they eventually do decide to address it. In many ways I had even less of an excuse than many, given that I was going out there encouraging people to adopt habits that I was eschewing myself.

Anyway, part of this sweeping-along process included falling into a relationship with my then partner, Jess, who'd first heard about me from friends who'd watched my appearance on the *This Morning* show in 2016.

Jess, who was a few years older than me, had once been an early-years manager at one of the schools in The Meadows. Although we both lived in the same area for a time, strangely we didn't know each other. Anyway, some time after the *This Morning* TV appearance a few of her friends tried to put us in touch because everyone in our neighbourhood was bigging me up saying 'Well done, Jacob' – and this news was all over Facebook feeds and the like.

I sent her a friend request after her mates attempted to set us up, and initially we only communicated via online chat. What made things a little more complicated was that by the time she accepted the friend request, Jess had moved to Dubai for a couple of years to work and had quickly manoeuvred herself into a senior role at a chain of nurseries looking after wealthy expats' kids – a situation that was worlds away, in every sense, from her job in The Meadows. So we agreed that we'd get together for the first time in person when she returned to the UK for a fortnight. And sure enough, when she came back, we went on a couple of dates in Nottingham and everything went really well. I was attracted to her confidence and charisma; she was flying high, knew exactly what she wanted, and appeared to be nailing her goals.

At that moment, I think we both wondered where it could all go, given that I was still living in a two-bedroomed house in The Meadows with my brother, hadn't finished university, was still doing freelance work on the side, and at the weekends was still going out drinking with my mates and getting off my head. There wasn't exactly a lot of room left for anything else in my life. Meanwhile, she was a seven-hour flight away and working all hours.

'You can always come out and see me in Dubai,' she said.

That was an invitation I didn't need to hear twice. Paying for flights using a combination of university money, cash in hand pay from removal jobs, and the small half-day rate I'd only just started charging for freelance consultancy work in schools and so forth, I started travelling back and forth to Dubai like a proper jetsetter. The truth is we were both pretty spontaneous people, so we were always going to have the best time in those early days, and we did.

From memory I went out there six times within the space of a year. I was basically a university student living two lives. While Jess was at work, I'd be mooching around Dubai in the sun. Then, when she finished for the day, we'd meet up at night and have nice dinners in hotels by the beach and go for long brunches at the weekends. For a guy who had hardly been out of The Meadows, I was loving this life.

Before too long, things got a bit more serious: Jess got pregnant unexpectedly. When I say that, I mean that we both probably knew it would happen, but neither of us seriously considered the reality, and the likely arrangements we would need to put in place as a result, until it happened. Suddenly, from being in a long-distance honeymoon-period relationship, we were faced with a real-life dilemma that had no obvious solution.

Because it's illegal in Dubai to be pregnant and unmarried, her employer told Jess that, technically, she could be arrested whenever she went to see a doctor – which of course she would have to do at some point in order to have routine checks during the course of her pregnancy. Not only that, she was also told that her health insurance wouldn't be valid for the same reason.

Realistically, given that it made no sense for me to move to Dubai, there was no alternative other than for Jess to leave her job and return to the UK for the remainder of her pregnancy. Things were getting real, and fast.

Looking back, each of us had our love goggles on and were trying to find the best set-up to deal with our life-changing news. It was both exciting and a little daunting that I was about to become a dad. Despite the complications, we simply trusted that things would work out; the relationship felt organic and absolutely right.

Jess was 31 at the time and I was 25, and I seem to recall she'd made references earlier to her body clock ticking that I either didn't notice or wilfully ignored because I was so caught up in the fact that I was in a loving relationship at all. I guess I was casually taking everything in my stride as I had done in the past, when I'd risen to every other challenge life had thrown at me. I just thought, 'This'll be no different.'

Did I want to settle down and have kids at the age of 25 after everything I'd been through in the previous five years? I don't really know. But would I just carry on and see where it all might lead? Absolutely.

I now know that that wasn't a particularly mature approach. But honestly, all I could think of was that for the first time in a long while I was relatively happy – albeit feeling increasingly overwhelmed.

As the pressure mounted and my mental health deteriorated, I remember asking Jess to 'just come home now.' Meanwhile, trapped as I was between wanting to lead a single life and thinking that being married and a parent was the mature way to go, I decided that the easiest thing to do was to try to do both for as long as I could. That was my not very considerate way of compromising, and for a while it worked.

Regardless of how happy I thought I was, I started feeling different kinds of pressures in the lead-up to the birth of our first child, Xander. Because I'd been travelling back and forth to Dubai so often, I ended up having to defer my final year at university because I hadn't got enough work done alongside everything else I was trying to balance: part-time job, long-distance relationship and so forth.

Meanwhile, Jess and I were organising her move back to the UK. We weren't doing what normal couples do when they're about to get married and have kids. Instead of going on dates, cooking dinners together with a glass of wine and thinking about just how to decorate our child's bedroom, I was still living something approaching a bachelor's life in a house with my brother, going out with my mates at the weekend and having fun. Meanwhile, she was in the process of leaving her job and clearing various debts she'd accrued while living in Dubai. This couldn't have been more different for us.

In late 2017, so many things happened – not all of them good. Shad Ali, my first mentor who'd introduced me to the Forgiveness Project, sadly passed away suddenly and his death really hit me hard at a point in my life when I didn't have much more capacity to cope with pain.

I've had so few positive male influences in my life – still less someone who operated in the same world as I did in the sense that he championed, through lived experiences, the power of forgiveness. Shad was a person I valued hugely both as a friend and as a mentor. To lose him so early in my rehabilitation journey, and when he himself was so young, did nothing for my fragile state of mind. After all, Shad was the first person I'd ever felt comfortable being truly honest with about my feelings.

In September, when Jess was back for a visit, we got married almost in secret at Nottingham Registry Office with just two witnesses: my brother and one of Jess's friends. Hardly anyone else knew. It was a bit of a whirlwind affair – and not necessarily in a good way.

Prior to our wedding day, I remember Jess phoning me from Dubai and saying, quite matter-of-factly, 'We'll need to get married.'

At the time, I knew it was a pivotal moment in my life – truly a fork in the road. But rather than taking a step back and weighing everything up, I was passive because I felt a little pressured into just agreeing. I never envisaged getting married under such circumstances. That said, I did make it clear that I was going to regard the marriage as exactly what it was: a means to an end in the sense that my child and his mum would be safe.

Once we were married, the floodgates opened.

Before I knew it, Jess was ordering all kinds of stuff online in Dubai for the little council house in The Meadows I was sitting in with Sam. For several days, random things arrived: curtains, furniture, mirrors and so forth. I remember thinking, 'Bloody hell, now the place really does look like a woman is living here!'

I just got swept along in it all. Don't get me wrong: as much as I loved Jess, there was a big part of me that thought everything was happening too quickly and I was panicking as a result. But I didn't have the balls to say so and I didn't want to offend Jess either – all of that's on me. The bottom line is that, unlike in my younger days, nowadays only I am accountable for the decisions I make or don't make. I gave up control by not speaking up – and again that's so ironic given that I'd gone through the uncomfortable process of restorative justice where one of the core messages is to speak up and communicate effectively.

The upshot of all this was that, by the time we actually lived together for the first time properly, after Jess returned from Dubai heavily pregnant, we hadn't really had a chance to establish what it would actually be like to live together in the same house.

Yes we'd 'lived' together, if you call me jetting into Dubai every couple of months for a holiday 'living', and the first few months of our relationship had been very rosy. But that had been in sunny Dubai, and in no way was that as real as sharing a small house in rain-lashed Nottingham with a baby on the way.

For one thing, since being in prison I feel like I've had a sort of mild OCD. Everything has to have a place, and I need order and structure in my life to not feel anxious and stressed. Knowing what my plans are for any given day, exactly where a bit if admin is filed, or where a specific hat or tie is located are important. But who wants to bring up whatever weird behaviours you may have right from the beginning?

When you swap palm trees on the beach for rain and The Meadows, only then do you really discover someone's traits and habits, good or bad. It's only when you're with someone all the time and living real life: arguments, crying babies, bills to pay and such like. I have seen many relationships fracture and break down during those first few years of having kids. There is nothing that can really prepare you for what's to come. Fortunately for me, the woman with whom I was embarking on this daunting journey had vast experience of young kids and, thank God, she was very well prepared for becoming a mum. Wow, was she good!

To say that it was all a bit stressful and daunting would be an understatement, and I'm sure that Jess, although she was older and more experienced, was having these feelings just as I was.

What did help was that, by the time Jess came to live with me my brother had moved out. While Jess and I were starting our relationship, he'd got into one of his own with his now-partner, Kurran – who at that time was finishing a university degree course in London.

While I was going back and forth to Dubai, Sam had been travelling to and from London for a few months visiting Kurran. When his course ended, Kurran then moved back to Northampton to live with his parents while looking for a job, and Sam eventually moved in with them too. This situation was extremely healthy for Sam because it gave him a surrogate family home situation that he'd never really had.

One major issue we had straightaway was, because Jess had been in Dubai for a couple of years, she wouldn't be entitled to maternity pay of any kind, nor was anyone going to give her a job while she was six months pregnant. Not just that; because she'd been blowing most of her tax-free money partying with other expats in Dubai before we got together, she didn't have much in the way of savings.

Right from the start, we were under financial pressure – which obviously isn't how anyone wants to begin a marriage. In addition, suddenly I had to adjust to the realities of being 'settled-down', a husband with a heavily pregnant wife at home, when a part of me felt like I still wanted to be going out with my mates now and again. That caused a lot of stress with Jess, who was saying things like, 'I didn't think it would be like this.' There was so much responsibility to adapt to and it all started taking a toll on my mental health.

In March 2018, Xander was born. It was a blessing having my little boy dependent on me. I loved getting him dressed out of his little clothes, feeding him his bottles, and letting him sleep on me for hours at a time (as opposed to putting him down and getting some housework done). He reminded me every day of how we all come from innocence – a blank slate. I have loved every minute of being a dad so far, and I love nothing more than being able to let my hair down and just being totally present with them. Planting and watering seeds in the garden, playing hide and seek, learning to read, walk and talk. What an honour.

But delighted as I was to be a dad, I still wanted to try and juggle the two dimensions of my life as much as possible. Now, it's one thing not being around when your wife is pregnant, but it's another nor being at home when there's a weeks-old baby boy in the house needing attention while your wife is exhausted.

Instead of just saying, 'I thought it would be different,' Jess was now protesting, and with quite a bit more force, 'I thought you'd be up helping me in the morning rather than lying in bed until lunchtime with a bloody hangover.'

She absolutely had a point. I wasn't being fair to her at all. But instead of discussing and working out a solution based on what we were both feeling, I just stayed out later and ignored the desperate phone calls, which were invariably followed by voicemails such as: 'Jacob! It's four in the morning. Where are you?' I simply didn't want to deal with the issue head-on.

This felt like the right thing to do when I'd had five drinks, but as the night passed and I started sobering up, often as the sun was coming up, I'd find myself thinking, 'For fuck's sake. I'm a dad. What am I doing?' My unhealthy coping mechanisms definitely were not serving my family well.

I'd sheepishly creep home, face the music, then, two weeks later, I'd do exactly the same thing all over again.

I went round in circles with this cycle for a few months until I finally realised that my going out drinking every weekend to block out emotions, rather than talking about why I was feeling them in the first place, wasn't helping me or my young marriage much. Before then, I'm not even sure I realised that was the reason I was drinking to excess.

But now I do. And the reason I do is that I reached the point where I stopped, looked back at my life and understood that, ever since 2011, it had been one life-changing event after another.

As hard as it is to admit, I think I was so belligerent in my early days of marriage and parenthood because, secretly, I was angry at having allowed myself to be funnelled into yet another situation in life that came with huge responsibility and the fear that I wouldn't be good enough.

The truth is that I hadn't processed the previous seven years sufficiently to be able to adapt to the present. So I owe massive thanks to Jess for bearing with me and doing a great job in diffi-cult circumstances.

There I was then. In no time at all, I'd gone from living in a bloody council house with my little brother to having a wife and a young baby. Understandably, perhaps, whenever I spoke to one of my mentors about how I was feeling, they'd say words to the effect of, 'Give yourself a bloody break. You are constantly jumping from one major life event to another.' And of course they were right.

I'm the kind of person who doesn't dwell on things I can't easily change. Everything that has been will continue to be. All we can control is the present. Instead, then, I close my eyes, in a figurative sense at least, take deep breaths and focus on controlling what I can actually influence. Although we've worked through some of our initial problems and I can't ever imagine myself being without Jess and the two kids we now have, I'd be lying if I said that our marriage hasn't had its ups and downs. That I see as realism. Having young children exposes even the smallest weaknesses in a relationship.

I do think that maintaining contact with your mates is an important and healthy thing even once you become a dad. I remember some of my mates who had kids very early on – they just got forgotten about eventually because they didn't come out anymore. I didn't want that to happen to me.

Back before I was married with kids, I tended to socialise with those who didn't have any responsibilities, simply because they were usually available at short notice when I rang them up to go out. Suddenly, I found myself in the position where, because it was assumed that I wouldn't now be available, nobody was ringing me up! For a couple of years, I totally resented that. It's not as though I felt like I'd never have any fun again in my life, but it definitely took me a while to come to terms with this, especially given I'd been one of the lads since forever. Unsurprisingly, that became a source of a lot of friction between Jess and me. Meanwhile, true to the cliché, my mates were saying, 'He's under the thumb now.'

As hard as it is sometimes to be a good husband, adapting to being a good dad was something I do take extremely seriously, for obvious reasons. I put this priority far above the need to maintain a relationship with my mates.

I decided at a very early stage that, no matter how rocky my marriage occasionally might be, I was always going to be there for my children (our daughter Tiggy is our second child) as a positive, consistent influence.

Dad has improved massively. Along with keeping up to date on the fortunes of Manchester United, we talk a lot more and see each other in person from time to time. I'm told that when dad was first told about what I did in 2011, he went on this massive walk somewhere and didn't speak to anyone for a few days – all of which is a typically male response, I guess. Then he came down to try and sort out Sam's living situation, while at the same time he urged me not to let what was happening shape the rest of my life.

I had to laugh inwardly when he told me this. On the one hand, it made sense. But on the other I couldn't help thinking, 'Well, thanks for that little pep talk, Dad. But where the fuck have you been for the previous 15 years of my life?' Anyway, I forgot about what he said as quickly as he'd told me. Once I was back among my friends and then went to prison, any momentary degree of positive influence my dad's words may have instilled just got swept away by years of negative beliefs and behaviours that his absence in my life had undoubtedly helped to reinforce. Meanwhile, he went back to Manchester. Our bond wasn't so good that I cared if I let him down anyway. He was miles away.

In the past I have resented my dad, and that's why I have had these important restorative conversations. I knew if anything were to happen to him, I would have always regretted it with him. If something was ever to happen to him, I don't want to be left with the torment of never having had the opportunity to get some difficult subjects out in the open.

I think one of my dad's primary issues is based on shame that he carries inside about not having been present in our lives. As a result, his dealings with me are probably underpinned by a fear of doing something that would upset me, thereby jeopardising the limited relationship that we currently have.

The unfortunate thing about all this is that when we are together, we get on remarkably well considering. In no way does it feel awkward. In fact, each time we are together it gives me a little comfort to acknowledge that we even have physical mannerisms and ways of speaking that are similar. You could say that our infrequent interactions are healthy, but they're also very safe.

To be honest, I have no idea whether my dad is even capable of expressing himself emotionally. Maybe his way of coping is to isolate himself in his own world; I respect anyone's methods of navigating their way through life. I've never even thought about it until I became a dad myself, which in turned made me analyse the origins of some of my own hardwired feelings and 'default settings'.

As I've said, because of my experiences at school, my coping mechanisms were either to tune out and daydream whenever anything stressful came into my head, or to consciously push the thoughts away altogether. As far as I can see, Dad's way of coping with life's struggles has been similar.

The crux of all of this is that when I had kids myself, the question I most wanted to ask my dad was this: 'You were in my life for seven years. Why didn't you try harder?'

Perhaps he was prevented from trying. The courts refused him access, but said he must maintain a relationship by sending letters. And he did send letters, I'll give him that much: I found a box of them recently when sorting through some of my mum's belongings. He also never missed a payment of child maintenance.

While he's definitely not the only dad who's been in this situation, and there are thousands who can say, 'Sorry son, your mum and I just didn't get along' or 'The courts stopped me from seeing you', it was having little ones of my own in my arms that made his actions hard to understand. Granted, he comes down to see me nowadays, not least because Jess and his partner have become good friends. Jess is forever sending them pictures of the kids and telling them what we've all been doing. It's those two rather than me and my dad who keep things going. But while women are often much better at keeping in touch, Sam and I just want our dad to make the effort sometimes – to ring us up and say, 'We're doing this.'

Equally, we both want him to have a go at us now and again too – to get in an argument so that we can have a normal parent and child relationship. I've never had a cross word with my dad in my entire life and that's just not realistic. In no way does it help a young man to get his own way all the time. When that happens in family life, it's inevitable that he'll then also push the boundaries of society.

Too many dads find themselves in the situation I described earlier where contact is so infrequent that they become afraid to lose what little they have. What they don't realise is that by being real, they will only gain. After all, nobody wants a parent who says 'yes' all the time for fear of losing contact with their offspring.

Even now that we're fully fledged adults all that Sam and I want from our dad is a solid dose of reality and consistency. Sometimes it feels as if my dad is just a parent of convenience. He parents according to what he needs and wants, not necessarily what we need. Having been away for so long, it's as if he lost the paternal instinct. But there's no question that my dad is a good man with all the right intentions. It has taken me this long to realise what makes him tick. I want a loving relationship with him.

Chapter Ten

Learning the Right Lessons

My upbringing taught me as much about how not to be, as how to be a parent. But the time I had as guardian to Sam, the effort I have put into repairing my relationship with my own father, and what I've learnt from education and lived experience of the criminal justice system have all helped inform the type of parent I aspire to be.

What really benefited me was the work I did going with schools of every kind, seeing kids who are like I was, and learning about how the dynamics that exist between parent and child have a tangible impact that has been statistically proven. And because of my understanding of these complex relational skills, I came to the understanding that the most important part of any child's life is the first four years.

During the earliest days of Xander's life, as busy as I was with finishing my deferred university degree course and doing the occasional programme for RESTORE in prisons like HMP Peterborough and HMP Isis in London, I wanted to be as present as I could be for my son and to apply as much of what I'd learned as possible.

Right from the start, because of my progress and rejection of outward expressions of violence and anger, I found it very easy to be loving and kind towards my son, and to talk to him softly in a way that I would never have dreamed I could, five years previously.

The truth is that many young men find it hard to let go of their machismo when they make the transition to being a parent. I'd matured, I think, so I didn't at all – to the extent that I'm sure a few people in my neighbourhood looked at me sideways when they saw me talking to Xander as I pushed him in his pram at the park, or carried him through the supermarket while murmuring gently to him.

As well as I think I've done, I'm sad to say that Jess and I have fallen short at times too. We have had quite heated domestic arguments in front of our kids and I'm not proud of that. It bloody eats away at me because, sadly, I have hazy memories of my dad mistreating my mum. I've never forgotten what I saw.

Oddly, it's one of the things I remember about the time before my dad left, other than disagreements about his plan to move north. I doubt my parents' relationship was ever very functional and it finally boiled over into violence. On the night Dad hit my mum, I remember trying to pull him off. I was only seven. At the same time I was screaming, 'Please leave Mum alone! Please leave Mum alone!' and we both ended up falling back onto the sofa.

When I let go of Dad, I thought he had calmed down. But he hadn't. He got up and continued throwing my mum around the room.

A neighbour must have called the police, and that, I believe, was the tipping point of their relationship. God knows how he wasn't arrested, but from there everything went down that awful path, which, while it's painful for the adults, is the absolute ruin of many young kids, me included: mediation, contact centres, divorce processes, absent dads, no male role models, and so on. Now I'm older he's acknowledged it, apologised. But it still happened.

All of this was on my mind whenever Jess and I got into arguments. In the moments where I found it almost impossible to control my own emotions when we were disagreeing, all I had was an image of me, sprawling on the sofa with my dad, trying to hold him off my mum. I shouldn't have had to go through that. No kid should. I'm certainly not repeating the mistakes of my own parents in front of my kids. Even though our arguments were just verbal, all I thought was, 'What damage could this be doing to Xander?'

Nowadays, whenever I catch myself being snappy or short with my kids, I stop and explain, always wanting to rectify the situation with a 'Daddy is really sorry for shouting. It is not your fault. I was being tired and grumpy. I love you lots.' All they want is my time and attention and they grow up so fast. So it's important for me to be careful in what I say to them. It's a blessing to watch their personalities blossoming.

In 2019 a producer for BBC radio, Victoria Ferran, contacted me about the idea of doing a podcast. From memory, I was at St

Pancras station in London waiting to get on a train when my phone rang in my pocket.

I liked the idea. Not only did I want to tell my story, but I also saw the podcast as a means of fleshing it out more generally by bringing in some of the practical applications that are related to the work I've been doing in schools, prisons, at restorative justice talks and in my degree, which I was awarded earlier that same year (first class honours).

To cut a long story short, I composed a brief proposal incorporating all of these ideas, and Victoria pitched it to Radio 4 for a five-part series, which was commissioned sometime in early 2020.

The plan was to work with a lady called Kim Normanton, a highly regarded freelance radio producer. As it turned out, she came to Nottingham just once and recorded me reading children's books to my kids, Xander and Tiggy, as an intro to the first episode. Then lockdown happened, and everything was up in the air thereafter.

As time passed, I was thinking, 'Oh my God, is this going to happen now?'

Rather than giving up on it, I decided I'd try and do as much as I possibly could myself. Given that it was my story, I thought I could do it. Not only that; because the podcast was also going to dig a little deeper into some of the wider social issues that I'd been tackling in my work since I was released from prison, I thought that it was possible for me to make the podcast happen, despite a worldwide pandemic and all the associated uncertainty and stress.

I was sent a Tascam handheld recorder, given a few basic hints as to how to test sound quality and so forth, and then off I went.

It wasn't easy finding places where there was no wind or echo. Further, because I lived in a small two-bedroomed house with a wife and two young kids, I knew that silence was going to be a rare commodity. In the end I discovered that my car was actually the best place to record: nicely soundproofed.

All the conversations I had with people for the podcast happened in my car and most took place while I was high. In order to get through the emotional stress of recording, my only coping mechanism was to smoke a joint before I started each session.

Depending on their views on weed, some readers might think to themselves, 'See! He hasn't reformed at all. He's still taking drugs!'

But if my smoking weed is the only means by which my rehabilitation is to be judged, then I would suggest that we as a society need to take a long look at what rehabilitation actually is and what we want from it.

One thing is for sure: if we're expecting perfection, we're going to be disappointed. The majority of people don't smoke weed and drink for laughs; they do it to block out emotions that they don't have the skills to deal with in any other way. And despite everything I've learned, I'm no different.

I'm not suggesting that drugs and alcohol aren't themselves a problem, because they definitely are. The line between recreation and dependency is a blurred one. But I think we've been trying to demonise these issues for long enough to no avail. Maybe it's time we started focusing on the problems in British society that make people feel the need to adopt these destructive coping mechanisms in the first place? Maybe we should examine why people resort to dealing drugs at all? How about that?

In the meantime, though, yes, I said it: I smoked weed during recording.

Recording the podcast was a welcome new role for me. For a long while, I had to take days off work (from house removals, delivery work for my father-in-law and such like) to honour commitments people asked me to make. It got to the point where, even though my mentors were screaming at me to charge for my time, for a good while it was costing me money to tell my story and to explore the associated social issues that it raised. I was coming to terms with the fact that while speaking about this part of my story so publicly, I needed to concentrate more on working in ways that would protect me better, that wouldn't simply continually open up old wounds, and that would be sustainable alongside my normal life.

The podcast made me realise again that, regardless of my past, I still had something new to bring to the table. Being in prison had not negated my value – and it shouldn't negate anyone else's either. The aim of prison should of course be to punish the perpetrator for a crime according to the guidelines, but that punishment doesn't need to continue indefinitely thereafter – or else we might as well leave people in prison forever.

I felt better about myself because I grew confident enough to acknowledge my own value. Being paid to do a podcast as a presenter rather than a guest was the culmination of that complex journey to being a practitioner.

All of this happened at a time in my life when I was considering stopping sharing my story altogether.

Jacob Dunne

As a result of the facilitator work I was doing in prisons, I was getting to a point where I wasn't enjoying it as much as I did in the beginning.

Instead of coming home buzzing about what I'd done during the day, I had started feeling a bit negative after a day's work in schools or prisons. While I might have been serving others, the work was no longer serving me so well.

In line with this feeling, I started to let things slip in my personal life. I became depressed, unmotivated, wasn't washing or taking care of myself with much self-pride. The sheer weight of all the life events of the previous eight years started to pile up on me and I was smoking more and more weed to escape how I was feeling.

Without knowing it was happening, I'd hit a point where I realised that I'd spent so much time and effort on other people that I, Jacob Dunne, had been left behind. I was regressing from the place of guilt I'd got to, back to shame version 2.

The Punch podcast therefore came at a time when I was starting to sink into a bad mental place. And I don't mind admitting that. Recovery from mental trauma is not a linear process. Adjusting to a new life is not easy.

But what motivated me most about this new venture was the reach the podcast could have. I liked the idea that it was to be on Radio 4 because I realised that those were the listeners I really needed to speak to.

I discovered this via experimentation of my own. When I was out delivering for my father-in-law's business in my van, I'd constantly be flicking back and forth between Radio 4 and BBC Radio 1Xtra, depending on what I wanted to listen to. When I needed serious information and knowledge – it was the former.

When I wanted some absolute bangers to sing along to at the top of my voice, I flipped to the latter.

I'd always thought, 'Let's get to the youth!' And with that in mind, my perfect audience for the messages I had to relay was something like BBC Radio 1Xtra. If nothing else, I'd be reaching the appropriate demographic. But what dawned on me was that these listeners probably weren't the people who could make any decisions about the social issues I was talking about.

For that, I needed to get to prison governors, teachers and leadership teams. I had to appeal to the individuals in charge of and responsible for the cultures for young people, as opposed to the young people themselves. BBC Radio 4 was a place to do that.

To fit this audience, I had to find the right blend of being gritty, compelling and informative. My hope was that it might lead to more freelance work in prisons and the like, while at the same time allowing me to subtly move away from telling my story, and towards more practical work, given that I'd just finished a degree and was looking for a new job anyway.

At the outset, when Victoria Ferran contacted me, I told her that, because David and Joan were always keen to be involved in bigger projects to raise awareness about the dangers of one punch and the merits of restorative justice, they might also consider being involved in the podcast if I asked them. So I talked to them, they agreed to take part, and the producer then took over the responsibility of organising conversations with them.

The process rolled forward, guided by the production team. Along the way, I was given help in my capacity as the podcaster presenter with scripting both broad narratives and also questions for the various guests who were called upon to contribute to the five, 14-minute-long episodes.

From memory, although I got a final draft manuscript of the content to review, I didn't actually hear the podcast all the way through before it went to air. As I reviewed the draft, I made very few edits other than to things that radio listeners might find difficult to understand.

For example, there was a moment when I let out a nervous laugh that jumped out at me straightaway. I recoiled when I heard it.

Not wanting anything to be misconstrued as disrespectful, I asked for it to be removed. On video, the reason for that laugh might have been clear. On audio, it could have been misinterpreted as flippant – which as I've said previously is the last thing I'd ever want with such serious and sensitive material at stake. No matter what, David and Joan's feelings have always come first.

I didn't have many expectations of *The Punch*. I thought I might get a bit of positive feedback here and there maybe, but honestly I saw the release of the podcast as the moment when I could let go of my story and move on with my life. I didn't think that anyone would have the appetite to hear anything more from me.

When the series was chosen as 'Pick of the Week' in some of the newspapers, in conjunction with Radio 4 trailing it on their shows as an advertisement, I started thinking, 'Hold on, this is actually gathering a bit of momentum ...'

Soon afterwards I was asked to do interviews with major newspapers like the *Daily Telegraph* and *Daily Mail*. Up until that point I'd been hoping that the podcast might just achieve what I'd set out to do: tell my story, explain the world of restorative justice and draw a line under my case for everyone involved. But when the coverage started to grow and I was contacted by an ever-increasing number of people who had been moved by the story, I realised that *The Punch* was much bigger than I ever thought it would be. As the pandemic hit, rather than it being the moment I finally put to bed the story I'd been sharing for five years, it was as if the world was saying, 'Hold on, actually we need more stories of hope like this.'

The rest, as they say, is history. We even won an award. I wish Mum knew that. Maybe I'll do another podcast one day.

Ironically, as much as David, Joan and I were further brought together by *The Punch*, its release was the moment when I simultaneously started feeling it was time to uncouple from them if I ever wanted to move forward with my life. I didn't want to be left telling the same story like a broken record on an endless loop.

To me it felt as though this was the logical moment, in the sense that we'd reached what felt to me like the end point of campaigning together concerning the story we were all part of. As important as it had been to deliver this dual-headed message – about how one punch can kill, but also the benefits of restorative justice – it felt like it was time for us to part ways permanently and leave any future communication between us as informal and optional.

Again, much as I was conflicted because of those feelings of shame and guilt, I just thought that, while I did want to continue working in prisons and so forth with a view to helping people like me, if I didn't detach from the specific narrative connected to James Hodgkinson's death, I would forever be defined by the night of 31 July 2011. I really thought I'd earned the right to transcend *The Punch*.

Now, some people are less charitable. To this day, even though roughly 90 per cent of the messages I get on social media are positive, I still get the odd one saying that justice for me would have been for me to rot in prison for the rest of my life. Obviously I don't agree with that, and neither does our judicial system. I served the sentence as per the guidelines; I had no option to do anything else.

Others might argue that to be forever defined by one event is my punishment for what I did. I don't necessarily agree with that either, but I am no stranger to this being a lifelong process.

I went to prison for what I did according to sentence set out by our judicial system. Not only that, I then went to enormous lengths thereafter to make whatever amends I possibly could for the damage I did that night. Whatever you think about prison's ability to rehabilitate a person, I think I've invested my fair share since into trying to make them work better. But I always knew that, no matter what I did, I could never bring James back.

So, as conflicted as I was in 2020, and as hard as it might have been for David and Joan to hear, I wanted to continue with my life.

When I thought about it more, I assumed that this was what they had always wanted for me anyway.

Throughout our relationship, they had clearly thought about the position I was in. When I was deciding to go to university, I remember Joan saying to me something like, 'Don't feel that you have to do this for us.'

At the time, that gave me pause to think. Maybe the doubts I was having were motivated by my guilt and shame, and had nothing to do with David and Joan at all?

After all, in a relationship like the one I have with David and Joan, everything is hypersensitive because, while I want to be respectful and engaged, and we do get along, I don't ever want things to become too casual and comfortable either. It's such a fine balance and perhaps I over-analyse things at times based on my own feelings.

In the end I had to make a decision and write a letter telling them how I felt. At the same time I told them that I planned to write a book, and I suppose even as I did that I was asking for their permission rather than looking at the plain facts, which were, as I've said already: by giving me the chance to engage via restorative justice and everything that followed, they saved my life. Now that I had that life, it made sense that I should live it on my terms. Maybe that's what they were thinking too?

This is just me theorising, obviously, but maybe because they had lost their son, they looked at me and thought, 'We can't bring our own son back, but maybe the next best thing we can do is help this young man, who has had few opportunities, along with his life?'

Maybe to do that was an extension of the healing they derived from the restorative justice process? Maybe I had no need to feel guilty about detaching? Perhaps being charitable to me gave them hope? I don't know these things, of course, and it feels like the moment to ask has passed. But I can't think of any other reason why two parents would extend such kindness and forgiveness to the person whose actions were responsible for ending their own son's life.

Chapter Eleven

Giving Something Back

In the aftermath of *The Punch* and my subsequent conversation with David and Joan, the majority of my work throughout the later part of the lockdown was in prisons like HMP Feltham.

What we are trying to do, via a pilot scheme that was set up by my amazing mentor Charlotte Calkin, is embed a six-week course in the prison system called RESET – which is entirely focused on the principles of relationships skills, restorative conversations and, most importantly given the type of people we're working with, conflict resolution.

This pilot isn't just aimed at the prisoners; it's also focused on the officers. We're trying to create an entire culture inside prisons where each 'side' speaks to the other in a way that de-escalates rather than promotes people triggering each other and kicking off.

Obviously, the end goal of this is not only to help people conduct themselves better in prison, but also to engender better behaviours to equip them for when they are released, with the hope that this new attitudinal reset will help them avoid the problematic cycle of reoffending and imprisonment – as well as giving them the skills to hopefully manage their own relationships better and make fewer bad choices.

The first pilot took place in HMP Isis in Thamesmead, southeast London, and it was a baptism of fire. Isis is one of the most notoriously rough prisons in the country, housing 18- to 25-year-old men who have committed drug-related and violent crimes – and everything else you can think of. Because it's in London, the prison population there is approximately 80 per cent BAME.

After the first day, Charlotte turned to me as we walked out the main door and said, 'Bloody hell. This is going to be hard. How do you feel?'

'No different to how I felt when I walked in this morning,' I said.

I'd been in prisons just like HMP Isis facilitating courses for the Forgiveness Project. I was confident that I knew what the attitudes would be and I understood all too well that very little effort had been made to educate prisoners and staff in the past with any relational skills. None of what we saw that first day was a surprise. Nevertheless, I still had hope.

On the second day, we walked onto the wing with renewed aspirations. Isis is a new-build designed in an old style with three levels, and as we appeared, this lad up on the third floor saw us and started shouting down the stairwell, 'Who are you? Who are you?' at the top of his voice.

If I'd been a prisoner I'd have probably said, 'Oi! Who the fuck do you think you're talking to?'

But I wasn't a prisoner with a number anymore, raging at the world. I was the new Jacob, on a mission to set the world to rights with straightforward and practical tools that everyone should and could use to their own advantage.

'I don't want to shout, but I want to come up and talk to you; is that okay?' I said to him, de-escalating the situation in a manner that wasn't so much *Straight Outta Compton* as straight out of my own developing restorative playbook.

'Okay,' he said.

When I got up there, he wasn't quite so keen on talking. And when Charlotte explained to him that we were going to be coming in regularly to chat about how we can have difficult conversations better, he looked even less comfortable.

'How do you think you are with having difficult conversations?' she asked him.

'I don't have difficult conversations,' was his response.

Then we told him that we were also going to be helping people develop good communication skills. His eyes lit up.

'I can communicate fine,' he told us.

Meanwhile I was thinking, 'Yeah, okay, a second ago you were shouting at us down the stairs. Sure, you can communicate!'

Evidently starting to feel uncomfortable with the silence that we intentionally let hang there, he said, 'Thanks, Miss', and walked off.

So that's what we were up against – and that's exactly why we were needed there.

How, though, do you get past responses like this?

Well, the first thing we realised is that to help people to communicate in prison, you've got to get them off their wing and away from their peers. Especially if you don't have much time to deliver interventions and are not working in the prison full time.

If you don't, they feel pressure to keep up their façade – a façade that is reinforced by the belief that it is weak and non-masculine to have conversations about anything vaguely emotional, especially with authority figures (even though we weren't strictly speaking authority).

Instead, you've got to create a safe space for conversations with individuals or small groups. Only then will you get the kind of engagement required to even scratch the surface of conflict resolution or effective communication skills. In the same way as I felt clarity when I was taken off the wing to pray in the chapel at Glen Parva, I hoped the same would be true with these young men.

The other major problem with prisons in the UK is that many prison officers are as bad as the prisoners themselves at communicating.

For example, on one of those first days doing the RESET course pilot, I heard one prisoner shouting 'Fuck your mum!' at one of the officers.

Instead of offering anything by way of de-escalation in return, the officer just got angry himself – to the extent that he got in the prisoner's face, shouting back, 'No, fuck your mum!'

Now obviously, conversations like that are going absolutely nowhere. No role model behaviour is being exhibited, but it's absolutely symptomatic of what's happening inside prisons every day in the UK. Everybody's shouting, nobody is listening – and in an environment where the attitudes are already very punitive, it's a recipe for disaster when prison officers simply take this 'It's my way or no way' kind of approach.

Thinking back to my time in prison myself, this attitude towards punishment in the prison population was always confusing to me. Prisoners – who themselves are being punished by virtue of the fact that they are serving a prison sentence at all – simultaneously have very extreme views about punishment that are at odds with social science.

For example, if you were to ask social scientists and facilitators working in prisons about how sex offenders should be treated, and then you asked prisoners, you'd get two completely different answers.

Facilitators and the like would probably say, 'Let's try to understand where the trauma that causes sex offenders to commit their crimes comes from.' Meanwhile, your average prisoner might say something more like, 'Shoot them. Kill them. Shoot them again. Then leave them in prison for eternity to rot.'

Granted, this is an intentionally divisive example intended to illustrate a point, but even when you go down to crimes of lesser seriousness, you'll still find that prisoners will come down on the side of harsh punishment more often than not, even though they feel like victims of the system themselves. There is something so ironic about not wanting to give other people a second chance, when actually what you yourself want most is a second chance.

These are the kind of ingrained cultural issues that exist inside our prisons, and the net result of it all is that, in terms of our conducting these courses, it's entirely possible that, in order to make any sustainable headway, we really need to spend as much time working with prison officers as we do with the inmates themselves. A paradigm shift of attitude and culture is required, and it's a work in progress that I'm still involved with now.

The truth of the matter is that prison officers can come from any walk of life. Lots of people only ever go into the prison service because it's an easy option. After all, you can get a decent salaried job with a nice pension, without ever having to do a degree.

Inevitably, that attracts people who really shouldn't be in the job of trying to relate to young people or adults with complex problems in the first place. Indeed, many of them have as many difficulties as the prisoners themselves. In my view prison officer training needs to be longer, more specialist and more interdisciplinary. The bare minimum entry requirement has got to be good communication skills.

At the moment, as long as you can complete the eight-week training programme, you'll be allocated a position at a prison and you'll have a job, even though you might have no relational skills beyond simply restraining people.

To me, that's just not enough training. You wouldn't employ a nurse who knew nothing or give a teacher a job without experience. Why do we do it with prison staff – especially when you take into account that the societal damage caused by imprisonment only heaps added pressure on the already stretched social care system?

Furthermore, while I don't know every detail of the training programme for prison officers off the top of my head, I know enough to say that, of the eight-week course, only half a day is focused on mental health. Given how big a part mental health plays in the issues of the British prison population today, that's a disgrace.

Thankfully, much as in any walk of life, there are good people in the prison service too. One of the women we worked with had grown-up teenage kids of her own and the reason she joined the prison service in the first place was so that she could learn more about the culture her sons were living in.

She talked to her sons constantly and therefore, when she came into work in the prison each day, she spoke to prisoners as she spoke to her own sons; her level of understanding was so far ahead of many others. Not only was she doing the job for all the right reasons, but she had also acquired the necessary communication skills to be able to talk to these young men without triggering them and making them feel offended. Equally important, she avoided getting caught up in her own ego and authority. Although her approach was the polar opposite of someone like my teacher Derek, she still created good boundaries that encouraged support and dialogue.

Ego is an issue with prison officers who don't possess communication skills, in the sense that, when communication breaks down, their ego engages and they resort to being overtly authoritarian.

As soon as it becomes 'It's my way or the highway', you're not teaching anyone anything and certainly not building any rapport. All you're doing is reinforcing these young men's beliefs that authority is to be mistrusted and, if need be, pushed back against. It becomes, I shout; you shout back. I hit you; you hit me back. It's such a vicious circle, and it's also applicable to parents, teachers and so forth.

I remember speaking to one officer on one of the wings in HMP Isis.

'Would you be interested in talking to us about communication skills?' I said.

'Nah, I'm not interested in any of that. I have my own way of doing things,' he told me.

All I could think was: how's that working for you when you're getting abuse and aggro all day long?

These people are always up against it because nobody respects them. Eventually, if they keep getting into arguments with prisoners, they'll get disciplined and ultimately sacked. The craziest aspect of all this is that there really is a culture within both prison staff and inmates whereby many love the drama and the possibility of regular conflict.

As you'd expect, staff retention in British prisons is terrible. They're training people more than ever, but they're also losing more people than ever. Why? Nobody wants to stay in the job – and to me that situation is as much a reflection of the quality of the training they're getting as it is down to the fact that the pay is enough to recruit people but not to retain them. The job is a day-to-day siege. From what I can see, they're being set up to fail. Something has to change.

What's the solution?

Conflict resolution and communications skills are the answer. Some people naturally have them, depending on what background they come from. They do well. The rest have no clue as to how to de-escalate a situation, and that's where people like me and other restorative justice practitioners come in.

Now, one of the things I was adamant about when I decide to talk about such things in a book was that I didn't ever want to come over as either authoritarian or preachy. After all, I don't have all the answers and this isn't an exact science.

Equally, I didn't want to bog people down in the science and details so much that I might as well have just published my Criminology dissertation and left it at that. Everything I'm saying is coming from my viewpoint as someone who has been at both ends of the spectrum. In equal measure I'm a cautionary tale and reluctant poster boy.

But I do have some ideas.

When I started moving away from just telling my story, as much as I could talk about restorative justice from my perspective, I still couldn't apply it, nor did I particularly understand it, from a restorative trainer's perspective. So I got more training in restorative justice practice and shadowed my mentors in the field, which, when combined with my lived experiences of restorative justice, meant that I was in a position to apply what I knew in the form of bespoke educational programmes with measurable results.

Not only that; because I had a third layer of knowledge in the form of my Criminology degree – which is the analytical dimension that allows me to think about my work in the manner a social scientist would – when I looked at it all on paper, I thought, 'I have quite a unique skill set here'

Reflecting on the educational resource programmes for young people that I was trying to apply, I couldn't help testing my resources and approaches against what I remembered of the 15-year-old me. I was a pretty good example of where everything went wrong.

There I was, struggling, labelled with conditions, disillusioned and frustrated. It had become this impasse, and the preferred solution of those in authority was to isolate me by throwing me in a classroom on my own and pretending I wasn't there. Before long, I pretended school wasn't there. Once I wasn't at school and was hanging around with other similarly disenfranchised and socially isolated kids, there was no saving me.

All in all, mine was a situation that really called for some kind of conflict resolution. But there was nothing like that available at all. Indeed, as I've said previously, the opposite was the case. Meetings about me took place without me in them. Nobody asked my opinion; nobody even considered whether I needed to buy in to any of these plans that were being made on my behalf. There was no attempt at resolution of any kind. I felt disrespected and out of control.

If somebody had said to me, 'Let's sit down, remove the emotion and talk this through', when I was 15 years old and angry, I'm not sure how I would have reacted. Initially, I reckon I might have resisted because that was my default position. But eventually I think I would have submitted to the idea.

Looking back, the thing that always bothered me about authority figures was the lack of consistency across the board. I had lots of teachers who took one look at me and said, 'No problemo. I'll soon sort this lad out.'

But as soon as things got difficult and I clearly wasn't changing my behaviour, they just gave up. When they did so, my disrespect for them – which was already at a high level just by virtue of the fact that they were the embodiment of authority – increased further. Rather than help me, they'd actually made the problem worse.

That's why consistency is vital to the kind of work I'm doing now. Everybody can have the best intentions in the world, but they've also got to be authentic. Lots of people just want to be seen saving the day, and then go on a victory lap – whether they're a schoolteacher, a prison officer or whatever – but when they realise that the problems they're trying to solve are too complex to be solved quickly, or they try to do too much and don't appear authentic, everything falls apart.

From my experience dealing with young men in prisons, the most important first step is to start slow with the 'I'm not judging you. Let's talk. I'm always here' approach, while still being firm and challenging them where I have to.

Essentially, with that approach, you make clear upfront that you're coming into the conversation with the best of intentions. That's one of many reasons why restorative justice has such a high success rate. Everyone knows what the agenda is and, because of that, everyone feels like they are getting something out of it. It's not enough to assume that the person you're trying to help knows that. Assumptions are the bane of effective communication.

There are a couple of tools I've learned that I've found to be invaluable throughout this part of my work. Bear with me here please, because I'm much better at doing things than explaining them. But I'll give it a go in a way that hopefully isn't too tedious. You might even want to try it out for yourself when the need arises.

The first concept is called 'The Social Relationship Window', and its aim is to ensure that you always hold whoever it is you are talking to at that moment to account and to make it easier to understand what category certain relationships fall into and whether they are working.

To visualise it, consider a square divided into four quadrants. In each quadrant, working clockwise from the top left, you have the words 'To', 'With', 'For' and 'Not'. 'To' represents a puni-tive/authoritarian approach; 'With' indicates a restorative approach and is the ideal place to be; 'For' denotes a permissive approach that ultimately helps nobody become accountable; and 'Not' corresponds to no approach at all.

The common approach I mentioned earlier, where someone does too much for another, is the 'For' position. It might seem like you're helping someone by working for them, but really you're making things worse because, by doing too much through trying to help, you're not letting them take ownership of anything. At the other end of the scale, when you work 'With' someone, which is the default position of restorative justice, it can make a real difference. Parenting and schooling frequently assumes that young people are not capable of these 'grown up' conversations. So often falls into either the 'To' or 'For' boxes – switching between the two with little success.

Often, it's the little things that matter. Using an example from my past, had I been included in any of those school meetings where schemes were dreamed up supposedly to help me, I'd have felt more valued and more included. That would have been work-ing 'with' me and the chances are that I would have responded better to that approach rather being treated like a child or, even, as a problem.

Equally, throwing me in a room for an hour with a teacher looming over me, telling me to read a book in silence, was working 'To' me, in the sense that it was punitive. And finally, the moment I was booted out of school so that I could become someone else's problem was the moment where 'Not' came into play in my personal story.

The other concept is the Parent–Adult–Child (PAC) model, where the ideal position to be in is the adult position. But in order to understand what that involves, it's important to first know how the other two positions manifest in real-life situations.

In the parent position, whoever is considered to be 'the boss' ends up in parent mode. Most people think that 'parent' is the best place to be, but the reality is that that's not the case.

For example, my mum spent most of her time in parent mode with me – and I fought against it all the way. Similarly, most of the teachers I had at school were in parent mode until I met Derek at college. He was the only one who operated in adult mode – not that anyone other than me responded to that particularly well at the time. Child mode is where there's no accountability and plenty of 'they started it'-type mentality. The important point to note is that all of us are capable of being in all three. Prison officers and prisoners, for example, are in child mode when they descend down the 'Fuck you. No, fuck you' route.

The key to all of this is knowing when to switch from one mode to the other. Life shouldn't be so rigid that a person stays in one mode all the time. We'd all be robots. It's about context, and knowing when to use a set of tools. That's a small point that I'd really like to get across, as I don't think anyone in the restorative justice world has ever explicitly made it before. I actually think it's what scares people off – the idea that you always have to be in one mode. That you have to turn your back on everything else you valued and thought. For example, I can still dress 'street' and talk 'hood': just because I learned how to communicate better doesn't mean I've had to become a Buddhist monk.

Knowing when to switch modes is all about self-awareness, and understanding how and when to just let your hair down and live. And these two concepts are intended to help us make this clearer to identify, so that we don't feel out of control.

For example, when we as an RJ team went out to the pub – as we did now and again after a hard day in prison – lots of the behaviours that I'd been teaching as part of my work earlier that day probably went out of the window. The reason? I'm in the pub with colleagues to let my hair down and enjoy myself. I don't need to worry about what mode I'm in (it's probably 'child' mode mostly!) because there is no need for a mode in that moment. I'm not teaching; I'm living. Like I said, it's all about context.

The other problem I've seen most commonly in prisons and schools is that the barriers between inmates and officers, pupils and teachers, are so ingrained in the culture that it's very difficult to effect change at all – still less, to do it quickly.

This, in turn, brings me to another observation, which is that, when people try to effect long-lasting social change, their expectations around how long that will take to work are completely unrealistic.

Because governments and, by extension, the bodies that work for them (prisons, school boards, health services, civil service agencies, and so forth) are dependent on people's support to be in power, it's inevitable that they look for quick results. If these results don't happen, their position of power is immediately jeopardised. But the truth of the matter is that long-lasting social change doesn't happen overnight any more than the problems that prompted the need for change did.

These things are generational – and so to make something as fundamental as a paradigm shift of culture work, there has to be a willingness to seed an idea and a culture shift in the right places, and then, rather than reacting when change doesn't happen tomorrow, wait and let the ideas propagate over one or two generations.

Patience is required in a situation like this, and that's a commodity that's in short supply nowadays in target-driven cultures. However, all I can do is hold myself up as an example of how it can turn out okay. As I've done many times in the last decade, we need to commit to what we want to achieve and then trust that what we're doing is right.

Across the board therefore, from where I'm standing, there has to be a willingness on both sides of every conflict to engage in trying to find a resolution. If we want to change prison and school culture (and this even extends into partisan politics), then both parties need to be involved in the conversation and move away from what is predominantly a discourse conducted in child mode that divides every conversation into left or right, good or bad, right wrong and so on.

Not only do both parties need to be involved and clear about what the intentions are, but they also need to be equipped with the right skills to have these restorative conversations that – in the specific case of politics – would ultimately pull everything back towards the centre.

The willingness alone isn't enough, sadly. Lots of people have the right intentions when they're trying to have a conversation about resolving something, but if they don't understand how the words they're saying might affect the other party, or if they make subconscious assumptions about them and what they know or feel, then the whole process is set up to fail from the start. From there it degenerates and the culture merely perpetuates. Kids get isolated from school and young adults get thrown in jail. Social isolation of any kind is where society falls apart and divisions grow wider.

Even now, with as much experience as I've had, I find myself walking away from conversations at times thinking 'Fucking hell, I so wanted that conversation to go well. How did it go so badly so bloody quickly?'

But at least I have the skills and the awareness to understand (a) that the conversation went wrong at all, and (b) why it did. From there I actually have a chance to make reparations in a way that's useful. If the cause of the breakdown of communication is down to me, I take ownership of that and articulate it as opposed to making up a reason and letting that relationship suffer.

Accountability is the absolute key to restorative conversations and conflict resolution. Until people accept accountability for their thoughts and feelings, it's very difficult to effect new communication habits.

People have often said to me: 'That's great, Jacob, but how do you stop people being triggered?'

That's a valid question – especially when we consider that we don't really have any control over how and why someone else might be triggered by something.

But the answer is very simple. First, we can be mindful of what things might trigger people and, equally, we can be aware of what our own touchpoints are so that we ourselves are triggered less. I'm talking about self-awareness here – and I'm speaking about it from the perspective of someone who has only recently acquired any because of my lived experiences. Additionally, when someone is triggered, it's best to avoid going into parent or child mode as a reaction.

A lot of this goes back to the ego – especially when we're talking about young people in schools, gangs or prison. It's all, 'He disrespected me', or 'He made me look a fool in front of my mates or my girl.' I myself once lived by those rules and, as we all know, I acted on them most of the time.

It all comes down to what our values are. 'Values' is a word that gets thrown around a lot. The fact is, if you sat most people down and asked them what their values are, they couldn't tell you. But if you analysed their behaviour: what pisses them off, what triggers them and what makes them act out, you can start to paint a picture of what those values really are and how they are controlling people.

A lot of the work I do with young people, assuming I get a long time with them, is based around establishing what their values are. I don't challenge them in these first sessions. Instead, I walk in, try to be authentic – and sit and listen with a willingness to see the picture develop.

I do so with the easier cases, and with some of the toughest possible nuts to crack. Eventually, when they understand that your intentions are good and that you're trying to help them be less emotionally triggered, well then you've got a chance to make progress. That's the joy of restorative ideas: blame in the traditional sense is removed in favour of accountability and practical solutions to move forward with.

Once you've broken the ice, it then comes down to your communication skills and willingness to relate to the other person's situation. From there you just look for a subject to build a conversation upon, and for me it was always easiest to use my background and upbringing as a way in.

I can even use the way I speak as a means to get someone to listen. I've been told often that I am able to switch back and forth between 'street Jacob' and 'facilitator Jacob', according to what the situation requires. I don't do this consciously; it just happens.

Obviously, it helps that most of the people I deal with come from backgrounds I can perfectly relate to: dysfunctional families; those with undiagnosed mental health issues; victims of poverty; and those who have been socially isolated in the sense that they've been excluded from school, been through the care system, been in prison or are living in a position of extreme poverty. In every case you're dealing with what presents most commonly as low self-esteem and anxiety.

Consequently, any time we can keep someone from falling into a form of social isolation, we're a step ahead of the game. Furthermore, we should be sharing the skills that stop people heading down some kind of self-destructive path.

To get anywhere with fixing society, with all of the above in mind, we have to consider implementing restorative practices into our schools first and foremost – to the extent that they almost become part of the curriculum.

Now, I know people, especially stressed and underpaid teachers, will say, 'Oh yeah, but we hardly have time to teach the curriculum we have, far less adding anything new.' I hear that all the time and I get it.

But I think maybe we need to have a look at what we're actually trying to achieve in schools with the curriculum we have.

And to do that we have to be really honest about whether six years of memorising information with a view to passing standardised tests is actually helping anyone when it comes to navigating a complex world. Unless you've drawn some decent cards in life and are lucky enough to live in a stable household, a GCSE in something like Physics just isn't going to serve you well in day-to-day life.

And while I have a degree, I'm not sure how well university equips young people for the realities of the modern world either. There's still room for improvement in a system where staff will bend over backwards to protect a university's ranking by making sure that as few students fail a degree course as possible. That helps neither students nor employers, who must recruit candidates from a pool of individuals with identical qualifications. Back in the day, if you failed a year, you were gone. Nowadays, universities are just giant cash cows that all charge 9K a year tuition fees to constantly increase student numbers. They are there to employ people and generate cash much more than to educate and prepare young people for life.

There is a lack of diversity of staff in universities these days. The majority of staff across social science disciplines appear to be left-leaning liberals. I went to uni myself with what you'd call liberal views, but there came a point when I badly wanted to hear other viewpoints and meet other people.

I think there are problems ahead for universities in Britain. We hold them up as these places where young people are meant to learn how to become independent, and that's fine to a point. But universities are in my view becoming oversubscribed, worse at delivering value for money for students in terms of face-to-face teaching, and less encouraging of free-thinking. Student enrolment fills quotas and generates income. It all seems a very expensive way for young people to get away from the family home and let their hair down. I still think schools should bear the burden of preparing us for life, much more than anywhere else – especially given that many of those who don't make it to university need this help the most.

We could do much better with education across the board, but especially in our schools. Some of the curriculum that we teach is bloody pointless in the context of what we're expecting young people to become. It's not kids' fault that they're being told what to think rather than how. I'm sure a lot of the teachers would agree. Yet we are basing our whole culture and model of social mobility on the GCSE system, which, though it has changed over the years, is still rooted in the past.

If we could seed restorative ideas in schools and workplaces and be patient enough to let the ideas trickle through over a couple of generations rather than pulling the handbrake after a week or a year, I think we'd get somewhere.

Meanwhile, in addition to cherry-picking other areas to focus on targeted reform, such as within the prison system, there could be general restorative messaging for the older population. By focusing especially on the young, the hope is that it becomes ingrained in the culture of schools, and then is taken home to the parents – a proportion of whom might well be resistant to such radical cultural change, but who also might just take some of the thinking onboard to support their kids.

From there I think we could effect a sustainable grass-roots culture change that would not only promote kindness and an aversion to conflict generally, but also help each individual to be kinder to themselves and less judgemental of others. It might take 15 or 20 years to bear fruit, but what's the alternative? Giving our kids the tools to cope with life without harming themselves and others should be a priority.

With this approach, nobody loses. Better attitudes lead to more self-aware parents who communicate better to form more stable family units and less socially isolated young people, fewer people in jail and a lesser burden on the prison system.

There has to be a willingness to fundamentally change what we're doing – it should be blatantly obvious that our current approach isn't working.

Chapter Twelve

Forward Thinking

I'm still doing my best to change society.

Am I perfect? No.

Is the communication within my marriage as healthy as it could be? Probably not.

Do I want to address all of these issues and keep evolving? Absolutely.

To that end, my marriage issues are my main focus right now. When all of us are happy, posing for a photo, having a group family hug, or simply sat having breakfast together to start the day off with a spring in our step, everything is perfect. That's what I want to work towards.

I'm just looking forward to facing the issues of each day with the tools and perspective I have. I've finally realised that I deserve that – as do my wife and kids.

What I've come to realise is that every parent is probably simultaneously still trying to process emotions from their own childhood. In that context, I think about my own mum a lot nowadays – specifically in terms of what she went through in her life.

Looking after Sam and I was just one of a number of stresses she had – and I wish with all of my being I could rewind the clock. If I'd had the knowledge I have now when I was adding to her problems by being entirely focused on believing that only my issues were important, life might have been very different. Our family might have had a chance.

When I was 16 and drinking and fighting, while simultaneously treating my mum very badly, I wasn't equipped with the understanding that I have now – aged 29 and myself a parent to two young kids. It's only because I've endured what I've been through that I understand and sympathise with how people either learn and adjust their behaviour to improve their lives, or they repeat the same mistakes and live an unsatisfactory existence – possibly with crime as a by-product of that, along with, in many cases, depression.

I could easily have gone down the latter path. I could easily be an absent father, in and out of prison with almost no rapport with my kids. Although I'm sure I'm past those tipping points now, there were several moments since 2012 when I could have unspooled everything I've achieved and ended up repeating bad behaviours and taking no accountability.

When I look back on things now, my mum had such a difficult life. It's very difficult for me to come to terms with the fact that she used alcohol basically all of her adult life to cope with her feelings of frustration and anxiety about life – not least the stresses associated with having to bring up two young boys on her own with few means.

Added to that, because she herself was adopted, I'm sure she already had her own issues from her childhood that she was still trying to manage by the time she became a parent. But what can you do? As human beings, especially if we're poor, we've just got to suck it up every day and carry the burden.

And my God, what an impact that burden had on her. Even before I went to prison, I sat in our kitchen and watched my mum drink. It got to the point where it was every night – largely because of the shit that I was pulling every day. God knows how much worse it got when I was actually in prison. I'm sure the worrying phone calls I was getting from my grandmother – as harrowing as they were – only told half the story.

In fact, not long after I got out of prison I found Mum down at the river's edge. I had to phone an ambulance because she couldn't walk. Her legs had stopped moving. Every night she slept on the sofa in all her clothes – and it's more than a little ironic to consider that, in the phases I've gone through when I've briefly stopped taking caring of myself, that's what I've also done: slept on the sofa with all my clothes on while my children were asleep in their beds.

The only difference was that I was high on weed and not drunk on Stella. It's so easy to let things slip. Simple things like brushing your teeth, shaving and making the bed are huge. Once you stop doing those things and being kind to yourself, you're in real danger of spiralling. I've been there, but thankfully I have pulled back each time.

Sadly, my mum never had the tools to pull back from oblivion – although I did try to get her medical help when it was obvious that her life was not going to end well. She never had the incentive to look at the ugly aspects of her true self in the way that my crime forced me to. It breaks my heart to consider that she held it together for years in impossible circumstances while Sam and I were growing up. Yes, she drank, but she also functioned and had a job that just about supported the family in conjunction with a few maxed-out credit cards. She did all of that for us, yet she couldn't save herself. She died far too young.

My going to prison was probably the last straw, I think. As difficult as things were in my teenage years, I'm sure there was part of her that thought, 'It's a phase. He'll get through it.' There is no doubt that she had huge faith in me.

But when I didn't – and her first-born son went to prison for manslaughter for a very public crime – her world collapsed.

Even though I emerged and engaged in the restorative justice process, it was too late; my actions must have made her proud but she was too far gone with the drinking, and her own self-worth was so irreparably impaired, that she just wasn't able to get past the idea that she had somehow failed as a mum and wasn't worthy of love herself.

I want to put it on record right now that my mum did not fail. In fact, by virtue of the selfless existence she lived in an attempt to give my brother and I a life like other kids, she made herself a hero in my eyes. My biggest regret is that, other than via the words of the poem I read at her funeral, I never found a way to express my love and gratitude for her. I didn't know how to and I was too busy thinking that the whole world revolved around my bloody problems. But I'm doing it now. So please, if this book can do anything, I hope it prompts you to give your mum a hug if she is still around or do something out of the ordinary for her. The little things really mean a lot.

I've only just about started processing my mum's death. For years her ashes followed me around. In the maisonette in The Meadows they were in a wardrobe in my bedroom. I saw them every day when I got dressed. In the house we live in now they are in a box that I can't even find. That's how much I'd buried the emotions attached to her passing.

But I'm going to change that. I plan to talk to Sam to discuss how we can respectfully spread her ashes in a place she'd like to be. At the same time we can both grieve properly, seven years after her death. As a single mum, she did so much for us. The least we can do is honour her memory properly.

On a wider level, I think single mums bringing up kids on their own deserve so much more credit than they get. In society, it's almost as if they are considered lesser beings and borderline vilified, while the dads get to walk away saying things like, 'The ball and chain didn't understand me' or 'The courts screwed me over.'

While there undoubtedly are situations in which good, well-meaning dads have found themselves on the wrong end of a bad marriage, more often than not it's their accountability that's missing.

Not being physically present does not necessarily mean you don't have to be accountable. If a marriage breaks down, as they often do, and parents separate and live in different homes or even other towns, that's not licence for one or other of those parents to let accountability lapse.

For once in my life I like myself. I don't feel as though I'm walking around on a tightrope 24/7. No longer am I ashamed of my traits. I no longer have hard and fast musical tastes either, in that I like all music, not just that which fitted with gang culture. Currently, I enjoy a bit of Freddie Mercury because he was one of my mum's favourites.

I'm kinder to myself – and hopefully, to everybody around me too.

Being kind to yourself is something that we hear a lot about nowadays, but I'm not sure if everyone views it the same way. In my case, when I'm driving around the country in a van doing deliveries for my father-in-law, being kinder to myself might be something as simple as pulling over for walks, particular in graveyards. It's a simple thing but doing that feels good and sparks my interest. I have not been sheltered from death and grief. So sitting in a graveyard actually helps remind me that we will all share the same fate. Plus how many other places have untouched wildflower meadows and ancient trees growing in them? I love architecture and local history too, so churches really are the the perfect places for me to take a break in my eyes.

It can be even simpler. In the winter of the pandemic, I found myself sitting on the sofa watching endless YouTube videos about nature. Even on a computer screen, in the depths of winter, it felt good to escape by watching clips about bacteria, termites, plants and trees. It awakened an interest in me. And when the weather improved and I felt spring was around the corner, I suddenly found myself gravitating towards real nature as opposed to just watching it on a computer screen.

Let me be clear: I wasn't just escaping my life by going into another one. Instead, I was merging these two worlds with a view to making myself feel better on a day-to day basis. It's an important distinction to make, I think.

Now, when I feel the stresses of life starting to build up, nature is my absolute go-to. Seriously, I can walk from the sitting room, out into the garden, and within a few minutes of just staring at a tree, I can feel like a totally different person. People probably think I'm crazy, but it really works for me. In nature, when the birds are singing, I'm at my absolute best.

Nature is so fascinating – so constantly changing and so deeply unthreatening in the sense that, unless we're talking about natural events like earthquakes, tsunamis and, dare I say it, pandemics, it doesn't actively engage with us. It just is. Better still, it's all around us if we care to look – even in the cities. We have access if we want it.

Nowadays, because it makes me feel so calm, I try to structure a lot of what I do around nature and my access to it. I might have had an argument with Jess and be angry and frustrated because of it, but as soon as I take the kids on a walk to the local park and start talking to them about the frogs in the pond, all my stress dissipates.

Not just that, but I'm showing my kids the things about life that motivate me in a way that educates them. Our rapport is great as a result, though if you'd asked me in 2012 if I'd ever have seen myself talking to children about the secret life of frogspawn, I would have bloody laughed at you!

Equally, when I'm out driving around the motorways of the Midlands and beyond in my van, there are inevitably moments where I'm tired, irritated by traffic or just simply feeling low about the fact that, despite everything, I'm still relying on my father-in-law for work. I'm massively grateful, though, to have been employed by him during the lockdown months, given that my prison and school work dried up. Regular income has allowed us to get onto the property ladder.

Whenever I feel a little dispirited, I look around wherever I am, find the nearest green area, park the van and walk straight there. I've posted impulsive videos of me on Twitter, where I've pulled off the M6, climbed the nearest hill and am shouting at the top of my voice about how great it feels to be alive and in nature. Whenever I can't actually get out of my van and walk around, I at least find I can recognise the types of trees I'm seeing by the side of the road or identify the crops being grown. My curiosity is endless when it comes to nature.

My Twitter followers probably think I'm deranged, and that's fine. I've found something about life that works for me, and it's my willingness to let my self-awareness guide me that's led me there. I really can say, 'Life could be so much worse than this.'

Obviously, when I'm driving around, I also see how much damage we do to our surroundings – especially in the more urban areas, where everyone is so far removed from that natural, calming environment.

This detachment has to affect people, even if they don't know it. I mean, look at how many people fell in love with gardens and allotments during lockdown. Surely that should tell us that, no matter what, we all have an affinity with the natural world that we need to engender if we possibly can. This kind of approach could sit hand in hand with the more restorative practices that I'm promoting via my work.

The problem, of course, is access. It's one thing being into escapism and curiosity, but if you don't have access to the things that you're curious about, the enthusiasm wanes or becomes diverted into something less gratifying.

I have given thought to what kind of initiative I'd like to put in place to help people beyond what I've done and will continue to do in prisons and schools. One of the ideas I had was to approach councils with a view to taking over specific areas that might have fallen into disrepair and turning them into green areas where people could just go and sit in nature – even within a dense urban sprawl.

Such relaxation areas, in which people can escape into a little oasis of nature even if they're in the middle of the city, are one of my passions. I'd like to leave behind a legacy of some kind – a positive footprint on my local area. I don't just want to be immortalised as that guy who killed someone.

Something else I've given a lot of thought to in recent months, while so much focus has been on mental health during the pandemic, are the diagnoses that I received as a child.

Honestly, for all that I used these as crutches to my own advantage, I never truly felt that I had anything that needed to have a label attached to it.

From a very young age, I just liked to escape in my head, especially when I was either bored or in a situation that made me uncomfortable. Was I alone in doing that? I very much doubt it. I think a lot of people go into their own head when they don't want to deal with something – especially when they're in a position where they can't just run away.

The other day I was recalling some of the conversations that took place in my house between my mum and my nan when I was young. The aspect I remember most is that there was a massive stigma around the idea of talking to yourself. It might have been a generational thing, but what I took away from it when I was young was that you were basically nuts if you did any of those things.

Ironically, a coping mechanism for me at school was to put things to the back of my mind and not acknowledge them. I'd even argue that my ability to escape into my own head made prison a lot easier than it could have been had I been present all the time. I have talked to myself and often had dialogues in my head over those years, and those conversations between my mum and my nan always stuck with me to the point that I did wonder if there was something wrong with me. Of course, I now know that it's impossible to think or evolve at all if you don't talk to yourself and others.

What I'm getting to is that I now think that my ADHD diagnosis only came about because they didn't know what else to call what I was doing. But it was wasn't a mental health condition really; it was simply me choosing to daydream or go absent in situations where it was easier to, such as in a classroom.

The ADHD diagnosis was in no way helpful for me. It set me up for a lifetime of problems. And the biggest tragedy of all is that it didn't even need to happen. If anyone had bothered to talk to me and establish why it was that I was checking out in lessons, I don't think it would have got to a point whereby my mum was so desperate for answers that she was willing to accept anything – including diagnoses that would hang around my neck for years of my life.

Interestingly, I have recently found all the correspondence that was sent to her regarding my conditions when I was younger. Apart from reinforcing how much effort my mum made to find answers and to help me, reading these letters really allowed me to revisit how I felt when I was much younger.

That's an enormously helpful thing to do; seeing the trail of history in writing reminds you why you feel the way you do.

My point is that we are far too quick to label young people with some fancy-named condition or a series of letters. Sometimes the cause of their problems is brain chemistry, or even something simpler such as a nutritional deficiency that could be easily addressed with better diet and supplements. It took me until I was aged 19 to establish that the diagnoses that I'd been lumbered with when I was 14 years old really shouldn't have been hindrances at all. If anything, they should have been tools to help me better understand myself and how my mind works.

If a kid isn't concentrating in the classroom, the chances are it's due to them not being able to concentrate because they've got other more pressing problems than learning the subject they're being taught – their mum drinks 10 cans of Stella after dinner, or their dad throws their mum around the house, for example.

Instead of vilifying these kids or slapping them with some potentially erroneous diagnosis, there should be scope in archaic curriculums to embed certain restorative practices that might actually be able to help.

Only recently, I realised that, in the same way as my mental health diagnoses didn't help me much, the deformity I was born with was also a much more significant factor in terms of its impact on my self-esteem than I ever gave it credit for.

I was born with the birth defect *pectus excavatum,* whereby my breastbone was submerged. What this meant in real terms was that I had this deep, painless indentation in my chest in the place where the breastbone connects to the ribs on either side. This dent was noticeable and for years I was very self-conscious about it at school, especially when it came to getting changed for gym class and games lessons. I was already quite an anxious kid by the time I became aware of this properly. Some of the reports that came back from school mentioned that I was always fiddling with my hands – a nervous habit, presumably – a stress reliever that helped me cope.

As time passed, people made fun of this breastbone issue, as kids tend to do, and it got to the point that the only time I'd ever take my top off was when I was on holiday somewhere with my mum, when I knew that I'd never see any of the people around me again.

After multiple visits to the GP about it over several years, it transpired that this condition is common in both men and women, but the difference was that, in men, because they don't have breasts, it's much more obvious. In 2008, when I was almost 16, I had to have a procedure to put a piece of metal – a titanium bar – in my breastbone area to support it and to stop potential damage to my heart and lungs.

To do this they had to break my breastbone completely, while I was under a general anaesthetic. They perform this surgery when you're younger because they know that you'll continue growing. In my case, I was told I'd have to go back in three years, when I was 18 or 19, to have the bar removed.

Well, I was in prison when I was meant to have this removal procedure done, and I just kept putting it off thereafter. Even though I knew it would have to come out, I didn't fancy another operation. Instead, I just put up with an increasing amount of chest pain, and this birth defect simply became another thing on the list of things I could fret about at that time.

For 10 years I found reasons not to have the surgery. And the longer I left it, the more paranoid I became. In 2008 I had the first part of the complicated medical procedure done. I received a huge boost of self-esteem when I saw that my chest looked normal. Eventually, in 2018, with a bit of encouragement from Jess, I plucked up the courage to go in and have the second part done. And when it was resolved, I felt a huge sense of relief, knowing I would never again have to worry about it.

During lockdown, even though our marriage often skated on quite thin ice, Jess and I went all in together on a mortgage to buy a bigger house just outside Nottingham proper.

Until the day we physically moved, I completely underestimated the wrench it would be to uproot the family from the place where my brother and I had fended for ourselves in the immediate aftermath of my mum's death. The process of packing boxes as I sat on the living room floor brought home to me just how many memories and aspects of the area I was attached to.

Now that we have moved and acclimatised to our new surroundings, I feel much better. Not only is the house bigger, with more room for the kids (a bedroom each) and a garden, but not having to drive, on my way to work every day, past the house that my mum, nan and aunt used to live in is a relief.

As much as I love The Meadows and the role it and the people in it have played in my life, it was definitely time for me to move on. The way I look at it, I've come so far that I can never stand still, far less go back. All I can do is keep pushing forward while always trying to be better. The alternative is unthinkable.

What's important is that I'm trying to improve. I'm currently doing so with the help of anti-depressants, which is itself a big thing for me to admit. As you know, for far too long I believed that for anyone, chief of all me, to admit they didn't feel mentally well all the time represented failure.

In my case, given that I'd been in prison for the crime I committed, that belief was even more extreme. For such a long time I just thought I had to be beyond whiter than the whitest of white. Anything less would have suggested that I was something other than totally reformed and the perfect citizen – especially in the eyes of potential employers or indeed anyone who was thinking about giving me a chance.

In my head, I always found it hard to accept the idea that, given I went out and got off my face with my mates now and again, I could also be the guy doing good things and helping people the next day. I thought one negated the other; I now know that's just not the case.

While I'm happy to take the majority of the responsibility for why I felt like this for so long, I do think that society's idea of what it means to be reformed is far too closely tied to perfection to be realistic. What does 'reformed' truly mean? How is it measured in terms of its value to a safe society – especially when you consider how many crimes of all kinds go completely unpunished?

The truth is that so many young people get a lucky ride and don't get caught committing crimes. And then they end up living a completely different life to the one they would have lived had they been churned up in the grinding gears of the criminal justice system.

On a wider level, and I tread very carefully and respectfully here when I say this, but what is it that I'm supposed to be reformed from when you really boil it down? As I've said, I didn't intentionally set out to kill James Hodgkinson. Yes I was fighting, as I often was in those days, but to end another person's life was not a wilful act on my part. The reality is that what happened that night on 31 July 2011 was unintended – though I want to make it clear again that I am totally and unavoidably accountable for the fact that I made the choice to throw an unprovoked punch that night.

What happened thereafter was entirely dictated by law: I was arrested, went to court, sentenced according to a set of guidelines and sent to prison. Did I need reforming from anything in particular? That's not for me to decide. But I do think there's an argument for saying that in many cases it is aspects of a person that need to be reformed or rehabilitated as opposed to the whole person.

Nowadays I don't feel that I need to demonstrate every day that I'm reformed. Instead, I look back on all the little phases I went through – insecurity, suppressing emotions, shame, guilt, doubt and the like – as just a part of my journey in life. I don't feel as though I'm being projected towards a Paradise-like place where I'll arrive as this perfect being. I'll simply continue through life, navigating the ups and down, hitting potholes, perhaps falling back on negative coping mechanisms, such as weed or booze, from time to time, but with the understanding that all of that is absolutely okay and that I'm probably not alone.

In a nutshell, as I sit here today I feel a lot more secure about who I am, and I'm totally comfortable with being seen as an example. I got out. I have made something of myself. While some of my old acquaintances are jealous of me, there are an equal number who have congratulated me at various times and said something along the lines of, 'Respect. You made it out.'

I know what my principles are and, significantly, that principles aren't rigid – especially not in a case like mine where I've had to change so much. I'm wary of getting too comfortable in one set of values, because I know what can come from that. After all, it was my getting comfortable with the skewed values of gang culture that led me down this path in the first place.

Today I just try to be open to everything – especially to acknowledging my own shortcomings or where my subconscious biases come into play in daily life. A combination of factors have led me to this position.

The first was studying psychology, I learned how to think outside the box and how easy it is for anyone to make bad choices. I could then apply that kind of analytical thinking to whatever I did day to day. I just can't stress how invaluable that was for me.

Second, I was forced to acknowledge the absolutely worst thing I've ever done – that my actions led to the death of another human being – and because of that everything else seems so much less significant.

Instead, I can just crack on and take everything in my stride. This life is a massive journey that I'm on. And I know that the moment I think I've reached the end of it is also the moment when I've probably become too rigid again. So I'm just going to go with the flow and see what comes.

To help navigate life I keep a daily journal of my thoughts and use a couple of mantras, the first of which is: 'I have a choice'. When I say that phrase as a mantra, the point I'm essentially reinforcing is that I have a choice regarding what response

I make to any stimulus; a choice, that is, of what reaction I have to it. It inspires me to take back emotional control in any situation that leaves me feeling a bit overwhelmed or impulsive.

The other mantra – which I'm sure sounds really soft and cheesy – is, simply, 'be kind to yourself.' For me that's the only way forward.

Appendix

6 April 2017: Notes taken on the way home from a day inside HMP Feltham

'I would rather feel safe and uncomfortable, than feel comfortable and unsafe.'

Could it be that our neighbourhoods stand at a point where our young people have become comfortable feeling unsafe on the streets they call home?

This young man expressed that he no longer wants to remain in situations where he feels unsafe. Unfortunately, he has grown up in an environment where feeling unsafe is normal. A few others also agreed with me in my discussions, but my fear is that many other young people have become so accustomed to feeling unsafe on a day-to-day basis that making the changes necessary to remove themselves from feeling unsafe is too big of a change to make.

Surely the reward of feeling safe is a good enough reason to change and perhaps sacrifice a few things? But let's think and try to understand what change looks like for these people to feel safe.

Perhaps they need to leave their family home?

Or go back into education, training and employment?

Move to a new neighbourhood, city or town? Try to be more confident? Leave close relationships behind?

Overcome prejudice and discrimination?

Change their fashion and their verbal and body language?

Get into a better routine, and develop self-discipline?

Understand what was causing them to feel unwell, and hurt?

Ask for help?

Find something they enjoy and can stick to?

Be driven by a different set of priorities and values?

To feel a sense of belonging to somewhere else?

To recognise unhealthy habits, and then create new ones?

To get a roof over your head?

To overcome the stigma of making mistakes?

To overcome the impact you have had on others?

To repair broken and damaged relationships?

To forgive yourself?

To feel alone and to step out of all that you have known so far in the hope that life just might be better on the other side.

Change varies, but some types of change ask us to look at the possibility of changing everything. We are guilty as a society of not trying to at least understand this process of change. We tend to choose punishment, blame or revenge as our first response to problems – which ironically is how our young people are currently treating each other and with devastating consequences.

This young man who shared this thought with me identified that he wanted to feel safe and was willing to put himself outside his comfort zone and feel uncomfortable in the process. However, do we expect him to do it all alone? Does he even have the capacity and support to do so? How can we play our small part in making change feel even slightly more comfortable for those who want to change?

As it stands, he and thousands of others remain out of sight and out of mind from those of us who could make change possible. There is amazing work being done by so many across the prison estate, but they too are carrying more than their fair share of the burden. This is a problem that affects everyone in one way or another, so if you are able to, try and understand by walking in the shoes of another, to respond with not necessarily empathy, but instead with basic rationale and objectivity.

For decades we have had little meaningful public debate about the best way to respond to crime. We have been told that the only way to deal with crime is by 'being tough on crime', so much so that we are all now experts on criminal behaviour and how to deal with it. As far as I can understand, this approach is underpinned by little proof of success. Reoffending rates are unchanged, the prison population has been increasing, and the levels of violence and suicide in prison continues to reach new heights.

Another young man in my discussions said that there was no difference between his life on the streets and the one he has in his community. We have adopted an approach where we expect prison life to be harsh, to be unpleasant – and therefore act as a deterrent for those who are convicted to its walls.

But despite the extremely unsafe and desperate conditions many of our prisons have inflicted, we have people living as prisoners within their own communities – where life is just as bad on the outside as it is on the in. It shows that both communities and prisons have been deteriorating at a dramatic rate. For too long we have over-policed and under-supported our young people. Generation after generation are passing down the trauma, habits and lifestyles to blame for the problems we face. With each generation becoming further embedded in 'the cycle of crime'.

It is a cultural issue, rather than a criminal one, and we are happily ignoring decades of facts and evidence, or simply do not care. Surely we will not just wait to become the next victim of crime before we decide to care? Sadly, even those who are the most affected by crime are often left feeling unheard and unrepresented. They are told that the criminal justice system will take care of the problem, and that justice will be served. It's time we discussed what type of justice will serve us better?

Is it about inflicting pain, getting revenge?
    Finding out the truth?
    Understanding what went wrong?
    Feeling safe again?
    Protecting the public?
    It not happening again?

Or people learning from their mistakes?

Justice can take many forms, but the current system rarely offers anything other than a punitive form of justice. How can we adapt our justice system to better serve everybody that is affected by crime?

It's true that hurt people hurt people, and revenge seems for many to be an instinct rather than a conscious choice. This is not just a debate about crime, but a debate about how we process our emotions, communicate our problems and move forward with our lives.

Would we accept healthcare policy that helps only a very few people, and often makes the conditions worse? Or accept an education system that teaches subjects and views that are not evidentially supported?

These young people call home a place where feeling unsafe is normal, where they are filled with anxiety and trauma from the life experiences they have witnessed. If we don't become serious about our concern for the welfare of our young people, the amount of violence and loss is only set to increase. It's time that we openly discussed the facts, and became accountable for having a serious rethink about how we respond.

I have a question for you: where did you learn how to deal with feeling hurt? And where did you learn how to treat people who have upset you?

The answer is society, the media, news, school, family, friends and faith. We learn lots from our communities and some of that stuff often needs revisiting. This is what the young man I spoke to was willing to face. He was willing to try and change his life in order to feel safe, but what has he learned by growing up in a place where feeling unsafe is normal? How long does it take to reverse this? And do we as a community have an obligation to assist with this challenge?

Fortunately, I see wisdom and bags of potential in many of the people I work with. That is because within all hardship there are lessons to be learned if we are open to see them – and if we are open to self-reflection and taking responsibility. Are we asking those in custody to do this, while remaining unwilling to do so ourselves?

The resilience and energy of our youth is the strength that is preventing even further tragedy. The sight of a young person with the weight of the world on their shoulders is a sorry one. The fact that change has become so uncomfortable and alien to these young people is a damning representation that 'the rest of us' or the 'non-crime-committing' among us are failing to portray a better alternative.

It is time we began to set an example, to do what we are asking of others ourselves, to show that taking responsibility is rewarding, that changing can be meaningful and better.

Postscript

The Change
I Wish to See

From my experiences I have drawn some lessons I think might usefully be applied by politicians and practitioners in order to address some of the challenges I have encountered in my own life.

Societal change
- I would like to see widespread training in and implementation of Restorative approaches to resolving conflict, whether that be in the workplace, the community or public and social services. Such approaches would replace outdated punitive procedures that often do little to change behaviour or repair harm.

- There should be wider public discussion around what justice looks like, and how our criminal justice system can better serve the needs of both victims and perpetrators.

- I would like to see a public health approach to tackling violent crime. Most of the prison population have complex social and psychological needs, and that needs to be recognised and responded to.

- Prisons should become places that prepare people for life back in the community – focusing on education, training, employment and restoring positive social relations with family and friends.

- For public services and communities to do all they can to keep connected and invested in families and young people who are at risk of being marginalised and excluded into unhelpful the arms of dangerous groups and doctrines.

- For restorative justice mediation to be used more in divorce proceedings.

Education
- There should be greater emphasis in the school curriculum on developing the soft skills needed to support young people's transition into adulthood and the wider community. These must include:

  o How to be more emotionally aware, objective and reflective in their thinking.

  o How to recognise and understand anxiety and manage emotional triggers better.

  o Developing the tools to resist unhealthy social influences and maintain boundaries.

  o How to navigate social media without the risk of harm.

o   Forming coping mechanisms for processing stress.

o   Understanding how to deescalate conflict and make better choices in 'the heat of the moment.'

o   Learning how values are formed and how they shape any given person's behaviours and views.

o   Educating young people about what healthy relationships look like and how they are sustained.

- We must prioritise teaching young people how to think. We must not assume that every family household will nurture these 'basic skills'. These skills are also particularly important in the digital age.

o   Where social media algorithms are becoming more and more manipulative in how they compete for our attentions and data.

o   The correlation between suicide and mental health issues amongst generations growing up online.

The standard of public debate

- I would like to see less divisive rhetoric between political parties, and more objectivity and balance within the printed press.

- I would like to encourage more people to understand the difference between facts and opinions. So that they feel safe to say 'I don't know enough about that issue to have a strong opinion.'

Acknowledgements

Where does a man like me start when it comes to giving thanks? So many people have supported me, challenged me, kept me grounded, and pushed me out of my comfort zone – seeing my potential and worth long before I could.

David and Joan, James's parents, were the catalysts for my renewed hope, and I will always admire the courage they showed to contact me and hold me to account. They are a shining example to us all in how to rise and face life's challenges; to transcend conflict into something better; and perhaps most simply to talk more with each other. However, conversations like ours take a great deal of preparation and sensitivity to prepare and guide – so I must thank equally Nicola and Jan from the charity Remedi for facilitating and leading our Restorative process as well as they did. The same goes for all the trained practitioners and charities across the country helping people find peaceful resolutions.

I must thank my mum and Aunty Paula for their consistent and unconditional love, and for all the lessons their lives have taught me. I am grateful to my dad and Janet for their encouragement and support when I needed them most. But also for just being there, at the end of the phone, in a house that was always open to me, and that has and will continue to be a place of sanctuary and respite. Even more so as their grandkids get older.

Big thanks to my brother Sam for preparing me early on for when my own kids become teenagers, but more recently for simply being a really good friend. He shares my love of history and nature, sometimes for hours at a time over the phone. I'm very proud of the man you have become.

I owe so much of my personal and professional growth to Shad Ali. He taught me to be kind to myself, and was my first real mentor and my biggest supporter. Shad, I miss you lots.

Special mention to The Forgiveness Project – to whom Shad enthusiastically introduced me, and with whom I still work passionately alongside. Especially for the time I spent developing my facilitation skills in prisons with the ever-amazing Sandra Barefoot. Again – Marina, Rachel and Sandra – thank you all so much for your continued support, and your determination to continue sharing stories offering alternative responses to conflict.

The Longford Trust, which helped me when universities refused to admit me because of my criminal record. We went on to play a key role together in reforming the admissions process, and you continue to champion education as a means of supporting rehabilitation. Peter, Phillipa and Natasha: thank you.

Charlotte Calkin is another priceless mentor with whom I have worked in just about every type of institution. Long may it continue!

Paul Hamilton, my tutor at Nottingham Trent University: thank you for helping me leave uni with an actual degree.

Thanks also to Hugh Shiel and Chris Gilzeane, formerly of Nottingham Youth Offending Team, for giving me the push I needed to start believing in my ability to help others and to imagine a better future for myself. I hope I have done you all proud.

To Mark Eglinton, for believing in this story and helping me put together this book when it would have been impossible to produce alone – thank you. I am hugely grateful to my agent Charlie Brotherstone for guiding me through the publishing world and the continued support he has shown throughout this whole process. And my thanks also go to the team at HarperNorth for seeing the value and the importance of the book, working with me to get it just right, and of course for giving it a great home.

Finally, I am eternally grateful to Jess: for putting up with the parts nobody else sees and for being the best mum to our children, Xander and Tiggy, who both have continued to teach me more about myself than anything else I've done.

Harper
North

Book Credits

HarperNorth would like to thank the following staff
and contributors for their involvement in making
this book a reality:

Laura Amos
Hannah Avery
Fionnuala Barrett
Claire Boal
Caroline Bovey
Charlotte Brown
Sarah Burke
Alan Cracknell
Jonathan de Peyer
Anna Derkacz
Tom Dunstan
Kate Elton
Mick Fawcett
Nick Fawcett
Simon Gerratt
Monica Green

Tara Hiatt
Megan Jones
Jean-Marie Kelly
Steve Leard
Oliver Malcolm
Alice Murphy-Pyle
Adam Murray
Genevieve Pegg
Agnes Rigou
Florence Shepherd
Zoe Shine
Emma Sullivan
Katrina Troy
Phillipa Walker
Kelly Webster

For more unmissable reads,
sign up to the HarperNorth newsletter at
www.harpernorth.co.uk

or find us on Twitter at
@HarperNorthUK

Harper
North